TOO SAFE
FOR THEIR
OWN GOOD

TOO SAFE
FOR THEIR
OWN GOOD

HOW RISK AND RESPONSIBILITY
HELP TEENS THRIVE

MICHAEL UNGAR, Ph.D.

McCLELLAND & STEWART

Library and Archives Canada Cataloguing in Publication

Ungar, Michael, 1963-
    Too safe for their own good : how risk and responsibility help teens thrive / Michael Ungar.

ISBN: 978-0-7710-8708-0

    1. Parental overprotection. 2. Risk-taking (Psychology). 3. Responsibility. 4. Child rearing. 5. Child psychology. I. Title.

HQ769.U478 2007   649'.1   C2006-904282-9

We acknowledge the financial support of the Government of Canada through the Book Publishing Industry Development Program and that of the Government of Ontario through the Ontario Media Development Corporation's Ontario Book Initiative. We further acknowledge the support of the Canada Council for the Arts and the Ontario Arts Council for our publishing program.

The epigraph on page v is reprinted with the permission of Scribner, an imprint of Simon & Schuster Adult Publishing Group, from *Jonathan Livingston Seagull* by Richard Bach. Copyright © 1970 by Richard D. Bach and Leslie Parrish-Bach. All rights reserved.

Typeset in Celeste by M&S, Toronto
Printed and bound in Canada

This book is printed on acid-free paper that is 100% recycled, ancient-forest friendly (100% post-consumer recycled).

McClelland & Stewart Ltd.
75 Sherbourne Street
Toronto, Ontario
M5A 2P9
www.mcclelland.com

1 2 3 4 5   11 10 09 08 07

"Why, Jon, why?" his mother asked. "Why is it so hard to be like the rest of the flock, Jon? Why can't you leave low flying to the pelicans, the albatross? Why don't you eat? Son, you're bone and feathers!"

"I don't mind being bone and feathers, Mom. I just want to know what I can do in the air and what I can't, that's all. I just want to know."

"See here, Jonathan," said his father, not unkindly. "Winter isn't far away. Boats will be few, and the surface fish will be swimming deep. If you must study, then study food, and how to get it. This flying business is all very well, but you can't eat a glide, you know. Don't you forget that the reason you fly is to eat."

Jonathan nodded obediently. For the next few days he tried to behave like the other gulls; he really tried, screeching and fighting with the flock around the piers and fishing boats, diving on scraps of fish and bread. But he couldn't make it work.

It's all so pointless, he thought, deliberately dropping a hard-won anchovy to a hungry old gull chasing him. I could be spending all this time learning to fly. There's so much to learn!

– Richard Bach, *Jonathan Livingston Seagull*

CONTENTS

AUTHOR'S NOTE:
THE CHILDREN AND THEIR FAMILIES

In order to protect the privacy of all the individuals with whom I have had the privilege to work, the reader must know that the stories I share in these pages are both real and imagined, based on bits and pieces of lives lived, cobbled together from anecdotes common to the many young people and their families whom I have met through my research and clinical practice. Each of the composite sketches of youth and their families that appear are substitutes for individuals whose identities must, of course, remain confidential. None of the people portrayed actually exist as I describe them, though some readers might think they recognize in these pages someone in particular. I would suggest the resemblance is more coincidence than fact. Perhaps, if the stories sound familiar, it is because throughout my career in a number of communities, big and small, I have met hundreds of youth who shared much in common. My hope is that readers find here stories that ring true for them.

PREFACE

I'm a social worker, family therapist, and teacher. My work has given me the opportunity to visit with troubled children all over the world: children who throw stones in Palestinian refugee camps and unsupervised teens on Israeli kibbutzim, children who dodge gunfire to go to school in Colombia's poorest mountainside communities, and those who live as student paramilitaries in remote parts of India, teenaged mothers living in the cinderblock slums of rural Tanzania, glue-sniffing children on native reserves in Canada's Far North, and bored disenfranchised youth existing in monochrome suburbs across the United States, Canada, and Europe. In many ways, these children are not all that different from one another. They are all at risk of being harmed or harming others, living desperate lives that force them to find creative ways to survive. And survive they do. The world over, young people tell me the same thing: they will do whatever they need to do to convince themselves they are competent, capable contributors to their communities. They are all, in one way or another, steadfastly committed to making their lives better.

For these children growing up amid real danger, our task is simple. We need to give them safer homes, safer streets, immunizations, connections with adults who won't abuse them, and most of all, hope.

However, for many other more fortunate children, I've become concerned that we are offering them *too much safety*. Odd as that may sound, there is a connection between all the security we offer children and why our kids behave violently, do drugs, and take risks with their bodies, minds, and spirits.

What's going on? Why would a child with everything choose the life of the delinquent, the bully, the runaway, the street kid, or the drug addict? Why would a child with everything insist on taking on responsibility that parents know is beyond her years? Why would a young person insist on being sexually active, or demand the right to work after school, threatening the grades he might get if he focused more on his studies? This book presents some unconventional wisdom to answer these questions, wisdom that comes from the kids themselves. They tell me that, whether growing up with lots of advantages or few, they crave adventure and responsibility. Both necessarily come with a sizable amount of risk. And both are often in short supply in families and communities dead set on keeping their children too safe for their own good.

Don't get me wrong. I am as concerned as anyone about our young people growing up and drifting into problem behaviours. But I'm worried that we may, out of our deep and committed love for our children, be overdoing it. It's not that our commitment to raising healthy children is the problem. It is simply that we are going about keeping our children safe in a way that is inadvertently putting them at much greater risk of serious harm.

The problem, at least according to the kids, is that they must search hard these days to experience any appreciable amount of danger or responsibility that makes them feel more like adults. This is a good news, bad news story. On the one hand, it is a testament to our collective success as parents. Fewer children than ever before are being injured riding bicycles. We vaccinate more, and sanitize their play spaces. We plasticize every sharp edge. We make it easier for them to stay in school. We educate them better about sex and help them to protect themselves. We tell them about the dangers they'll face if they smoke or do drugs.

And we've been successful in getting our message across. The statistics tell us our children are physically safer than ever before. Fewer children are hospitalized for accidents or childhood illnesses, and fewer must suffer with debilitating diseases.

The news is just as good for our children's minds. Fewer children today drop out of school or have unprotected sex. The rates of drinking and driving and of suicide have declined. All those years of early intervention with neighbourhood watch programs, crisis counselling, peer mediation, non-violent conflict resolution, stay-in-school programs, teacher training, youth outreach workers, urban reclamation, mobile libraries, after-school activities, anti-abuse campaigns for little league coaches, police checks, better certification for swimming instructors, and programs to help our children say "No!" to predators, to drugs, to smoking, and to sex has all added up to a much safer world for our children.

SO WHAT'S SO GOOD ABOUT RISK-TAKING?

But how much of a good thing is too much? While we are keeping kids safe, have we also paid enough attention to some of the good things that risk-taking brings us while growing up? Can you remember a time when putting yourself in harm's way was a rite of passage you craved? I remember those large steel playground wheels I used to love to jump on and spin around on at high speeds when I was a kid. Emboldened by the adrenalin rush of centrifugal force, my friends and I wouldn't stop until our stomachs heaved. My city council recently voted to remove them from my children's playground. I'm becoming anxious that we've gone *too far* in removing "risky" activities from our children's lives.

After all, once we've taken away all the dangerous things for our kids to do under our watchful gaze, where will they turn to find their thrills? We mustn't forget to offer them other opportunities to experience moments of growth and exhilaration.

This book explores how to find a balance between keeping our children out of harm's way while still offering them what they need to experience the thrills that are part of growing up. My message is simple:

- First, as parents and caregivers to our children, we need to be vigilant when real risks exist, but ease up when our fear gets the better of us. Well-founded worry conveys to children they are loved; senseless, ungrounded worry debilitates children in ways far worse than the few bumps and bruises they may experience without us.
- Second, when children do act out and put themselves at risk, we need to force ourselves to listen to them closely so they can tell us why they have chosen to take more risk and assume more responsibility than we think they can handle.
- And third, we need to provide children with safe substitutes for their risk-taking and responsibility-seeking behaviours that can provide just as much excitement as they find when they put themselves in harm's way. These substitutes must help kids feel like adults in ways that are meaningful to them.

In the workshops where I bring these ideas to parents, I am often chided with a chorus of "But our children are *safe!*" I hear beneath the rebuke the testimonials of parents who are deeply concerned for the welfare of their children. We adults must, of course, offer our children every possible advantage a safe and secure life can bring. But when most danger is absent, we must ask ourselves what else we could offer our children that brings with it the adventure and maturity they associate with risk-taking and responsibility-seeking behaviour. I'm not against removing senseless dangers from our children's lives, but I hear all too often from children themselves that *something is missing* when their lives become too safe.

Our children say we worry too much. Maybe, just maybe, they are right.

The problem is that children are at a loss to find ways to be powerful people. The media have convinced us that the world "out there" is dangerous. We believe we are being quite sensible to pull back and shelter our kids, and we answer each of their requests for more adventure and responsibility with "No," or "Wait until you're older." But with or without us, our children won't wait and they won't accept "No" for an answer. We hear stories about piercing and tattooing, and about the sexualized behaviour of young girls. We are anxious about our kids surfing porn sites on the Web, about violence on the playground, and about them using drugs with names we can't even pronounce.

This book is about our children and the deep-rooted psychological need for risk-taking and responsibility-seeking that underlies the maturing process. I will show that children who push to find their limits (and scare us adults in the process) may also be those who are the ones most ready for life.

• 1 •

THE RIGHT AMOUNT OF
RISK AND RESPONSIBILITY

Tom and Janice thought they had shown the right amount of concern. They'd given their daughter everything she needed. Now, at sixteen, Desiree was getting herself into big trouble. She had all but dropped out of school and would rant and scream at her parents if they tried telling her what to do. Tom and Janice were sick with worry when they finally came to see me.

It hadn't been like this for very long. Desiree had always been impulsive and awkward with people. Her parents had helped her find ways to stay involved with other children, driving her from one sporting event to another, their car doubling as a taxi most evenings to ensure their daughter was part of everything. Tom coached her summer soccer team so he could watch her. Janice made Desiree's birthday parties neighbourhood events. The little girl coped well and managed some success, both at school and on the playground. Tom and Janice were happy to be their little girl's life preserver.

Only, the little girl grew up. By sixteen, she no longer fit the life jacket her parents had made for her. Desiree couldn't make her high-school soccer team on her own. Her friends began to think her strange. Hanging out with Janice wasn't a substitute for peers. Soon Desiree became argumentative, surly, and started stealing from her mother's purse. She became demanding as well. When she went

1

shopping with her mother, Desiree would call her names in front of store clerks at the mall. She would refuse to wear anything that didn't come with a huge price tag. When she earned her licence (her parents paid for her driver training course), she insisted on taking the family's second car anytime she wanted. When the car developed a dangerous gas leak, and Tom hid the keys to protect his daughter, Desiree said he didn't love her and ran away for two days. Nothing Tom or Janice tried seemed to be keeping their daughter safe.

Nor could it.

Desiree was finding out that she was on her own and sinking. Scared, and without much practise finding her own way, she was a girl at risk of choosing drugs, the street, or an early pregnancy as a way to cope. After all, those choices are always near at hand and compensate for feeling lost and lonely.

Tom and Janice did nothing wrong. They did what we would all do. They had cushioned their daughter from life's blows. If that had been enough, Desiree would have grown up fine. However, once safe, children like Desiree also need opportunities to fail, and to fail often enough to learn how to pick themselves back up. All our efforts to promote self-esteem are horribly misguided. Children need to know their limits and how to bounce back. Desiree needed both a life preserver and a sailboat. If she had had both safety and adventure, love and independence, she might have been better able to cope as a teenager. She might have been more ready to navigate her way through the rocky course of her development.

Working with the family, I encouraged Tom and Janice to set limits for their daughter, but also provide opportunities for her to make her way on her own. My message was clear: "You've done your job! Now it's time for Desiree to do hers." Taking the keys away was the right thing to do. But insisting Desiree earn the money to repair the car and take it to the shop herself (and provide her parents proof that it was safe to drive) was what the girl really needed. It was a tough step for Tom and Janice to take. After all, Desiree was still their little girl.

Tom and Janice are typical of families who are driven by fear and who have the means to "bubble wrap" their children's lives. It is that fear that is stunting children's growth. We see the results all around us. Children who don't leave home until their late twenties, but who don't contribute financially or emotionally to their families either. Young people who, despite the opportunities they've enjoyed, still grow up troubled, addicted, and even possibly headed for jail, those without meaning in their lives, or worse, suicidal. A whole swath of our youth is feeling lost amid the sanitized, prescribed, regimented order of their too safe upbringings. These children tell me

Too much risk and we endanger a child. Too little risk and we fail to provide a child with healthy opportunities for growth and psychological development.

they have everything but what they need: opportunities to experience some measure of risk and responsibility, responsibility both for themselves and others.

OUR FEARS HAVE BECOME OUR CHILDREN'S PROBLEMS

The Russian educational psychologist Lev Vygotsky[1] wrote decades ago that all learning follows from experience. We simply cannot grow up without getting our hands dirty, without grappling with whatever it is that we need to master. A child who has never had to find her footing on anything but flat, safe ground will grow up clumsy. A child who has never had to make his way in a crowd on his own will grow up shy and unassertive. Vygotsky advises adults to provide children with what he calls "scaffolding," a supportive structure of opportunities. We do this by offering small, achievable challenges, served up one at a time, like rungs on a ladder.

In many communities, we are failing miserably at doing much more than keeping our children vacuum-safe. They are not getting the experiences they need to grow up well. An entire generation of children from middle-class homes, in downtown row houses, apartment blocks, and copycat suburbs, whose good fortune it is to have sidewalks and neighbourhood watch programs, crossing guards and playground monitors, are not being provided with the opportunities they need to learn how to navigate their way through life's challenges. We don't intend any harm. Quite the contrary. In our mania to provide emotional life jackets for our kids, helmets and seat belts, approved playground equipment, after-school supervision, an endless stream of evening programming, and no place to hang out but the local mall, we parents are accidentally creating a generation of youth who are not ready for life.

A concerned parent provides scaffolding for growth, not just a life jacket for safety.

GOOD PARENTING IN ACTION

The problem is that parenting is not an exact science. And kids don't come with operating manuals. What is a good risk for one child could be disastrous for another. What one child interprets as the actions of an overbearing parent, another will feel soothed and comforted by.

So how do we know how best to parent our children, providing them enough risk and responsibility without endangering them more than they already are? Periodically, throughout this book, I'll invite you to reflect on your parenting practices, encouraging you first to think differently about what your child needs, then asking you to try something new in regard to how you parent.

In the pages that follow you'll be introduced to many youth and their families. Some of these stories will be of troubled teens who do things far worse than your child has yet done. These stories, while all based on real kids, are meant to show only what *can* happen when children are too protected, not what *will* happen for certain.

What works for one family might not work for another. My best advice is to ignore all the professionals, myself included, and trust yourself first. Ultimately, the parent who is acting out of love and concern, who intends his child no harm and is willing to do what it takes to maintain a relationship with that child is the parent whose child will, on the whole, do well. Families are too diverse for there ever to be one recipe for success. Consider the following three families, each with a teenager who's using drugs.

THREE FAMILIES, THREE NEEDY KIDS

Family One, the McClellands, live in an upper-middle-class neigh-bourhood with neighbours whose lawns are all well-manicured. Values of church and community are strong, though you seldom see anyone outside on those lawns or walking down the sidewalks. The McClellands' two children are chauffered from one activity to the next. Both parents work, often longer hours than they'd like. Each of their children has their own television and ensuite bath. The family shares meals as often as possible, but the kids are just as likely to eat with their live-in nanny as with one of their parents. When drug paraphernalia appears in their fifteen-year-old daughter's room, the parents react by insisting Cassie attend counselling, signing her up for a twenty-eight-day in-patient program. Cassie complains that her parents don't understand. She tells them drugs are a form of self-expression for her. Besides, she says, "All my friends are doing it." She insists she's too smart to do anything involving needles or even any-thing harder than marijuana, hash, and some club drugs like Ecstasy.

For Cassie, doing drugs means being old enough to make her own decisions. It's about belonging to a crowd, and finding some adven-ture. It's no surprise she left the clues everywhere. This is a kid begging for someone to notice her and take her seriously. How else is she going to convince her folks she's old enough to make decisions for herself? Old enough to have some real responsibility (she doesn't want the nanny!), and desperately seeking some adventure. Pre-dictably, all that treatment does nothing. It isn't long before she's back home, yelling at her parents, breaking curfew, and selling her clothes for extra money. Now, most nights, her parents don't even know where she's sleeping.

The Kwongs live in a suburb a mile from the McClellands. Their home is a renovated seventy-year-old saltbox in what was once a working-class neighbourhood that now has become a thriving com-munity. They kept a close eye on their daughter, Shao-Lin, when she was fifteen, insisting she take music lessons and excel at school. They wanted her to go into medicine, though she herself hoped to study anthropology one day. Her parents insisted that the social sciences were not a good professional choice, but they let her attend a summer science camp at the local university, where she got to participate in activities related to both medicine and anthropology.

Her drug habit only came to light when she was caught shoplifting an MP3 player from an electronics store at the mall. It was the court-appointed social worker who told the Kwongs their daughter was going to use the money to buy alcohol and drugs for her and her friends. The social worker said she already knew many of Shao-Lin's friends. "Nice kids," she told the Kwongs. "Not into real serious problems, but not angels either." The Kwongs learned their daughter had chosen friends with far fewer rules than at their home, and with basement bedrooms where they could do whatever they wanted.

After that, the Kwongs cut off all contact between their daughter and her friends. No telephone, no e-mail. They insisted their daughter suffer all the consequences of her actions, going to court with her, then making sure she did every one of her community service hours. And they grounded her for three months.

Remarkably, the girl accepted all her punishments and stopped using drugs or drinking. She changed her peer group. She devoted herself to music, and her marks rose dramatically. Her parents were pleased with the change and forgot all about the mistakes she had made. The next year the girl consulted with a guidance counsellor about the courses she would need to get into medicine. Apparently comfortable with taking no further risks, the girl settled into doing what was expected of her, excelling at everything her parents wanted her to achieve.

At eighteen, and in her first year of university, she was referred to me following her release from hospital. She'd slashed her wrists but insisted she wasn't really trying to kill herself. The hospital kept her only for observation. Her biggest problem now was how to deal with her parents, who she was sure would find out what she'd done when she went home for Thanksgiving. The marks on her wrists would never completely disappear.

Family Three, the Pelletiers, also have a fifteen-year-old daughter. Lyne looks like she walked off the cover of a rock 'n' roll magazine: black mascara, dog collar, piercings, and a tattoo on her upper arm.

The Pelletiers live in a quiet rural community that they thought was a safe distance from the city. Their two older sons never got into any trouble, but they know their daughter is making up for what they missed. She used to be a very nice little girl whose room was pink with a collection of stuffed animals numbering in the hundreds. Their daughter says she is still just as fashion-conscious, only not in ways her parents understand. She still likes to spend time at home. She thinks smoking is stupid, but has no hesitation using drugs or drinking. She tells her parents everything. Her father, a plumber with his own business, and mother, who works at the local library, don't know what to make of their daughter. They give her most everything she asks for. Except the tattoo. That they'd said "No" to, but she hitchhiked into the city and got one anyway with the birthday money her grandparents had given her. Her father had been furious and driven the girl back to the tattoo parlour to see if the place was "clean."

Despite the occasional argument, the girl insists she has no problems. She's in school, holding her own. She has friends and is never ashamed of her parents meeting them. She doesn't drink at home and agrees to keep her curfew as long as her parents are willing to provide her with rides to and from her friends' parties. She loves to shock her family and dresses up as wild as possible for every holiday celebration. Her mother says she won't take her shopping at the Salvation Army, but every other week is happy to go to the local used clothing store, Frenchy's, and sort through the bargain bins. Her mother tells her daughter she'll buy her anything that isn't ripped or too sexy. It's a reasonable compromise. Sometimes, when there is something her mother won't buy, Lyne pays for her clothes with the money she earns every lunch hour looking in on an elderly woman who lives next to her school.

Your family does not likely resemble any one of these three families exactly. Or maybe it does. Either way, it's important to realize that Cassie, Shao-Lin, and Lyne are each reacting to a different family culture. Each have different strengths to draw upon, and each hears different messages about herself and her risk-taking and responsibility-seeking behaviours.

While each of the girls was asking for more risk and more responsibility, there is no cookie-cutter solution for how to provide them
with these experiences. Cassie wants to be respected as a young adult
and receive more attention from her parents. She wants them to see
her for who she really is, the independent child they made her. Shao-
Lin wants less attention, not more. She needs permission to be more
independent and make her own decisions. Children like her are
begging to be given the opportunity to take more risks and assume
responsibility. Lyne is far more reckless than she needs to be, but
then again, of all three girls, I'm the least worried about her. She
remains attached to her family and enjoys being with them. She is
community-minded and in many ways shows the maturity and other
personal qualities that reassure me she will do just fine in life.
Though she takes many risks, including using drugs, she's not letting
others influence her. She is the kind of outspoken, caring individual
who makes a great adult, even if she drives her parents crazy along
the way.

Do Something Different

Growing up, did you know any girls who resembled the three young
women just introduced? Imagine a conversation with one of them
now as an adult. How would she explain her behaviour? How risky
would have been risky enough? At the time, would she have said she
had a problem? I'm sure her parents would have said she did, but did
she think she had a problem?

It's the answers to these kinds of questions that help us tune in to
what our children are trying to tell us.

Try one of the following:

- Think about how your spouse would handle a situation with the
  kids and then do exactly as he or she would do. At least once. In
  my family, that would mean ensuring the kids put out the place-
  mats at every meal, with forks on the left and knives on the right.
  It would mean full meals served while we are all sitting down. No

on-the-fly grab-fests. That's what my wife likes. Dinners, with everyone in attendance. She has a point of course. It's not necessarily my way of looking at dinnertime, but I've learned that occasionally doing things her way has its benefits. If you don't want to emulate your spouse, try someone else whom you admire. The point here is to realize that there is no one correct way to parent.

• Invite your child to organize one aspect of your family's life. Just this one time. Let your son decide where the family will go for dinner Friday night, or maybe where you should spend your next summer vacation as a family. Don't agree to anything that makes you feel financially burdened or oddly out of place, but accept that you will feel a little uncomfortable just the same.

Doing these exercises is not meant to make you change how you parent. They are meant to help any parent realize there is no one correct way to raise a child or run a family. The McClellands, Kwongs, and Pelletiers all did many things right even though they each approach their roles as parents very differently. We are simply much better parents when we are flexible in how we do our job.

IT BEGINS EARLY

The challenge to find enough risk and responsibility begins early for many of our children. It seems the older my children become, the more difficult it is to know what to offer them. How much supervision is enough? How much responsibility? What is an appropriate amount of risk-taking behaviour for a twelve-year-old? What about a seventeen-year-old? Sometimes it's easy to know the answer. I can feel my way along, guided by both what I experienced when I was young and what my neighbours caution me to do in this day and age. Our son and daughter, aged nine and twelve, are allowed to walk to school by themselves, and can now be in the house for short periods alone, as long as they don't have friends over. Both take responsibility for the dog they convinced my wife and me to buy, though we share that responsibility with them as well. Our children have each travelled alone by bus to see their grandparents and once even flew without us when they went to see their cousins in Montreal.

Sometimes, though, the answer to how much risk and responsibility is appropriate is far less clear. Lately, as my children have grown, I feel on shakier ground when it comes to making good decisions. When I had two tickets given to me to see the Rolling Stones at an outdoor concert, I took my son, Scott. As a drummer, he loved the music, but the concert came with some risk. Or at least, perceived risk. There were teenaged girls walking topless with a thick layer of body paint (is he too young for this?), and in front of us a group of fortysomethings discreetly smoking marijuana. "Dad," my son asked me quietly, his mouth to my ear as we waited for the Stones to come on stage, "are those cigarettes?"

I told him the truth. It was an opportunity to talk about drugs and what doing drugs can mean, and what it doesn't mean. But nagging there behind the throbbing music from the six-storey speakers were bigger questions. Was this all too much, too soon? I know I'm not the only parent who's confused.

It wasn't that long ago that I was on the playground with my daughter, who was just seven at the time. "Don't go any higher," I remember hearing the mother of an adventuresome four-year-old tell her daughter harshly. She was standing a short distance from us, her little girl enjoying herself too much to listen. She kept climbing the brightly painted monkey bars shaped like the back of a giant turtle, their red metal tubes just the right size for little hands to hold. "That's high enough, Tess. You listen to me or we're going home *now!*" The woman's voice turned angry, determined to make little Tess do as she was told. I was there, just a few feet away, pushing my own daughter, Meg, on the swings. She urged me to "Push harder!" and I did, but not as hard as she would have liked. Meanwhile, little Tess had climbed higher than her mother could reach. But she wasn't yet at the top of the weblike structure. I watched as the little girl stopped her climbing but made no effort to come back down either. She just held tight, her little bum up in the air, two white sneakers planted firmly on the bars below her. She wasn't looking at her mother, but at her hands and then up to the last few rungs she still had to climb.

"Tess," her mother growled again, "you come down now." I realized the mother's voice sounded panicky. Not angry. Tess likely heard the same anxiety and she looked down, became afraid, and began to cry.

"I can't," she said and held tighter, pressing her belly onto the bars, making her less stable. Her mother threatened a bit longer, and then Tess, with tears gushing, backed her way down to where her mother could pry her from the bars and set her on the ground with a firm shake.

Staring from the swings, I felt sorry for both little Tess and her mother. And maybe even a little sorry for myself. I wondered when was the last time Tess's mother had climbed monkey bars? Twenty-five years ago? Her body, like mine, had no doubt long ago forgotten the exhilaration of balancing one's weight, the challenge of height, and the self-absorbed satisfaction of tasting danger close at hand. I remember these things more in my head than my arms and legs. It would likely be a while before Tess tried anything so risky again. The thought made me sad because my wife and I have cautioned our own children in just this way. I have Tess to thank that day for teaching me something important. The next time my daughter yelled, "Higher, Daddy! Do an underduck!" I grabbed her swing firmly with both hands, shouted, "Hold on tight," and ran full tilt forwards with the swing at arms-length, giving her an extra-high push as I passed right under her legs. Above me, Meg's peals of laughter were tinged with both a quiver of fear and unbound exhilaration.

THE 4CS OF SAFE AND RESPONSIBLE CHILDREN

There was a time our playgrounds were less supervised. Children were allowed to go down to the corner store and buy milk for their parents. Or cigarettes. That's the problem with looking backwards. There are lots of good things to say about how we were raised. We had more opportunities to experience challenge and adventure, and to carry the responsibility and expectations of our parents. But there were also lots of bad things about those times.

Somewhere in the middle there is a better way to raise children who will be *Competent, Caring Contributors to Their Communities*, the 4Cs of individuals who grow up well.

The competent child knows her talents and has opportunities to demonstrate them.

The caring child has been shown empathy and can express it to others.

These children use their talents and capacity to care as a way of making a contribution to others. That contribution not only brings with it recognition, it also provides a sense of personal power, known as self-efficacy. The child who contributes to the welfare of others knows he can change the world.

Best of all, demonstrating competence, caring, and making a contribution joins one to a community, however one defines community. A community is a group that shares a common identity or geography. A community can be as small as a group of friends or as large as everyone you meet on the Internet who shares a common interest (Trekkies, after all, think of themselves as a community). The child who knows himself to be a competent, caring contributor to a community is the child who is more likely to have a sense of place and purpose and to feel proud of who he is.

Here's the rub, though. Children I have worked with in mental health clinics, young offender facilities, schools, and in a number of community recreation centres have argued with me, and finally cajoled me into understanding that the most resilient and healthy among them are those who become part of a community, any community. When doors into communities that promote positive behaviour are closed, children choose those where the price of admission is less. Drug addicts, delinquents, partiers, and dropouts all provide just as much of a sense of community, purpose, and place as staying clean, out of trouble, and in school. These kinds of communities offer the experience of risk and responsibility for others as much as mainstream communities. Even the delinquent will tell you she feels a sense of loyalty to her peers. That same delinquent might confide that she likes the danger she gets herself into. Once we understand this, we are better able to decode the choices our children are making. One way or the other they are going to become integral members of a community. In ours or someone else's.

I've been a slow study realizing this. In fact, for the longest time, I felt that my clinical practice and research was supposed to show me how to prevent children from being around anyone with whom they would experience any appreciable amount of risk. Slowly and patiently, the youth with whom I have worked have shown me instead that they like themselves better when they can label themselves risk-takers and responsibility-seekers. When they succeed at both, they tell me they achieve the 4Cs.

Children confide that they like themselves best when they *test their limits under the watchful gaze of adults.* And under that gaze, they are that much more likely to succeed. And they know it! In other words, they would rather be contributors to the communities they share with their parents and caregivers than part of communities that get no respect from adults. But our children are unwilling to be innocent bystanders in the struggles of our communities. They want to participate. They want to be risk-takers and responsibility-seekers who play a part in the action, using their talents and demonstrating their capacity to care and cope.

Instead, many of these children and youth are told to sit quietly on the sidelines, to take no risks, and assume few, if any, real responsibilities for others. We adults think we're doing our children a favour by protecting them and supervising them. The kids have a different opinion altogether. Many vote with their feet, choosing troubled peers over proud parents as forums for self-expression and experimentation.

HOW MUCH SUPERVISION IS ENOUGH?

So how much supervision is enough? There's a groundswell of parents who are beginning to argue we are all just a tad too worried about our children's welfare. David Anderegg, author of *Worried All the Time*, describes the phenomenon of "helicopter parents"[2] in a recent issue of *Reader's Digest*. It's an apt term, capturing the way some parents fear disaster everywhere their child goes, so they hover, always close at hand. The question is, however, what does an adult's fear become for the child it burdens? Does that fear convey love? Or does the child feel the anxiety of the adult? Is the result a liberated child who is capable of caring for herself and others? Or a child stifled and restless? It would be a shame if parents ever stopped worrying. But all the time? And about everything? I'm not sure I could have borne up well under such scrutiny when I was a child. It's a shame really, that something so well-meaning turns into exactly what it doesn't intend to become. Love becomes that which a child must resist. Safety, something abhorred rather than coveted.

> Too much safety is not what children need. It's not what we adults needed either, when we were the age our children are now.

When our fears overly inhibit our children, the results are endless rebellion and the recklessness that endangers rather than develops young bodies and minds. But there are also others who suffer: the parents. A young man I know reflected on how doted upon he was by his mother. He sighed, and told me, "I wish my mother would get another project besides me."

HEALTHY PARENTS MAKE HEALTHY CHILDREN

When I meet parents who have the time to focus exclusively on their children, who insist everything in a child's room be just so, who have made their child their life's work, I admit to feeling a little sad. Sad for the child who will become either spoiled or overwhelmed; even sadder for the parent who will wake up one day with nothing but an empty nest.

And yet, I can understand the compulsion. We get used to being the all-knowing parent. The one with the food, the answers, the motivation, the transportation. We are our children's models. It is a role I, for one, would never willingly give up. It's just that as children grow, so too must the nature of our love. They start to look to us to model a healthy lifestyle that balances our personal needs with the needs of others. How we use our spare time will become their way of using their spare time, how we treat friends and relatives, how we look after ourselves and our relationships, the same.

The parent who ignores her own personal needs and sacrifices all for the needs of her child (assuming there is an abundance of other supports, as there are in many communities) is short-changing the child of valuable lessons in how to live life with balance and respect for personal boundaries. I often tell parents, "Take care of yourself, if not for your own sake, then for the sake of your child."

The healthier a parent is, the healthier a child is likely to be as well!

Ultimately, isn't a healthy parent one who models good ways of living? A healthy parent:

· Sets healthy boundaries in relationships
· Shows both caring for others and respect for his own needs
· Demonstrates calm in the face of crisis
· Takes time to do good things for herself
· Is firm about personal boundaries when others make demands

Such parents provide children with a gift far greater than a tidy room and a twenty-four-hour Net nanny. They provide a role model.

Writing in *Psychology Today*, well-known author and psychologist Hara Estroff Marano talks of America today as "a nation of wimps" and wonders why "Parents are going to ludicrous lengths to take the lumps and bumps out of life for their children"?[3] There has been an unprecedented number of college students who are now reporting anxiety and depression as their key concern rather than the relationship problems of a generation ago. What are we doing to create such an anxious bunch of kids? Rather than seek an answer we have simply done more of the same, cushioning our children even further. For example, grade inflation at universities is a growing concern. The university professor who bucks the trend is more likely to get an earful from an irate parent of an eighteen-year-old than the student who pulled off the Cs in the first place.

Of course, this is merely the latest in a long line of overprotective parental behaviour. The fourteen-year-old daughter of a family friend teaches swimming to elementary school-age children. Recently, she learned the ridiculous lengths parents will go to protect the self-esteem of their children when she asked an eight-year-old to repeat a swimming level. The child couldn't tread water long enough, or swim the one hundred metres required to advance to the next level. The child's parents would have none of it. They couldn't tolerate their child being "held back." It's as if this was a personal slight against them. Surely, I thought when I heard this story, if ever there was a place where there is little doubt whether a child is or is not ready to advance, it's in the pool. One's child either can do the front crawl for a hundred metres or not. To advance the child up a level is not just wrong, it's reckless and endangers the youngster further. Will she be a strong enough swimmer to survive falling out of a boat? A hundred metres from shore, will her self-esteem really be the issue?

When parents threaten, pool supervisors, and even university professors, give in. Parents win, but at what cost to their children?

FOR WHOSE SAKE?

So what's going on? Have we confused what's good for our kids with what's good for adults? Marano writes, in a related article, that for many parents, their children have become Trophykids,[4] the child's success a reflection on the parent's capacity as caregiver. One result has been an unhealthy amount of supervision. Adults go to great lengths to protect children from the very experiences of failure children *need* to grow up healthy.

Yes, this is a testament to the love parents feel for their children. Sadly, it is not going to reap the results parents seek. Real success for a child comes when the child follows her or his passion. In my counselling work, I encourage risk-taking and responsibility-seeking behaviours that, within bounds, help children to express their passion for life. I encourage parents to make strategic decisions about where to ease up and where to clamp down. I caution them to avoid squashing all that is unique and special about their children. It is a dance in which both parents and children are seldom moving to the same music.

That's a shame because our world doesn't need more people doing the same thing. We need innovative risk-takers who are passionate about charting the frontiers of their chosen professions. I like passionate young people:

- They make the best employees
- If they've been risk-takers and responsibility-seekers, they bring to their work great life experience
- They whine less when work gets difficult
- They have something authentic to say about their accomplishments (they don't have to exaggerate!)

It's these kinds of youth who are most coveted by employers. Responsibility-seeking, risk-taking is the very best way to prepare a young person for future independence and committed relationships to family, work, and community. It just needs to find appropriate outlets.

This success comes at a price for parents. We have to let kids experience some knocks in life in order to establish a healthy, well-grounded self-esteem that comes with looking a challenge in the face and pushing through.

THREE QUESTIONS

If you are a caregiver (parent, teacher, coach, or maybe big brother) of a child in a community that is reasonably safe, then I ask you to consider three questions:

- First, *What are you really worried about?* Our children today are in far less danger than ever before, and we have the numbers to prove it.
- Second, *What are you doing to provide young people with the rites of passage they need to become adults?* We can help our children grow up healthy if we provide them with opportunities to show

what they can do and the structure to navigate safely the period
between being a child and acting like an adult.

- And third, *What substitutes can you offer them?* Children who act
out in dangerous ways are desperately seeking risk and responsibility. It's up to us as adults to provide them with substitutes for
these behaviours that meet their need to be active parts of our
communities. In short, children are the safest when they are
exposed to the right amounts of risk and responsibility, in doses
they can handle.

SO, WHAT *ARE* WE WORRIED ABOUT?

What worries parents is very often exactly the kinds of experiences
children say they need to thrive. Like boats in the harbour, moored to
the dock, our children today may look nicer than ever before and
show great promise, but waiting idle at shore was never their purpose.
Everything we teach them is supposed to be making them seaworthy.

But we hesitate. Clinical therapist and M.D. Elizabeth Guthrie, in
The Trouble with Perfect, cautions us, "To develop a strong sense of
self, children must feel free to fail. This is a critical component of any
achievement. No one, child or adult, can succeed without being
willing to risk failure."[5]

The good news is that we live in a world where our children are
safer than ever before in recorded history. And yet, we are more overprotective now than even a generation ago when the world was a
much more dangerous place. Crime, teenaged sexual activity, drug
use, and high-school completion rates are all changing for the better
(see Chapter 6 for more details). Even if the numbers don't convince
us, reading Ann-Marie MacDonald's *The Way the Crow Flies* should.
Her account of small-town North America in the early 1960s is a
chilling portrayal of how much danger our children once faced. As
MacDonald shows, even good parents could refuse to believe their
children could become victims of sexual abuse, ignoring what good
sense should have told them and taking no action to protect them
from the obvious. There is no reason to idealize what is past. It is far
safer to be a child today.

The fact is that very few of us will ever experience anything close to the tragedy we see daily on Fox News. Researchers in the United States have shown that violence affects people in patterns.[6] Where you live, how your family behaves, your lifestyle choices, all affect your chances of being the victim of a major crime or assault. That means that for most of us, the risk of becoming a victim is very small. Furthermore, those who have experienced one violent event are the ones most likely to experience more violence – up to seventeen times more likely. All this assumes, however, that you are living in a high-crime district and even then, your lifestyle must still place you in situations where you are more at risk than others.

As much as we like to be afraid, the truth of the matter is that very few of us are at any great risk at all.

What middle-class kids are really at risk for is the empty feelings that come with not belonging, and with not mattering to anyone. When we deny our children opportunities to feel challenged, responsible, and proud of themselves, we sow the seeds for what the nineteenth-century sociologist Émile Durkheim called "anomie," the empty feelings that precede suicide. The truth is that *our children are less at danger from others than they are from themselves.* One in four North American teens meet the criteria for substance abuse problems or mental health issues such as depression, both linked to these feelings of emptiness. Yet fewer than one-sixth this number ever access the services they need. Suicide remains the second leading cause of death amongst young people aged ten to twenty-four, outnumbered only by traffic accidents.[7] This problem is serious, but its solution is as near at hand as our children themselves.

JUMPING INTO ADULTHOOD

When children push themselves to their limits, they make it more likely they will grow up to be capable, responsible, trustworthy individuals who know where they fit in. What is it then that has made us so fearful of our children's quest for danger? If we're honest with ourselves, most of us will admit that at some point we tested our own limits and worried our parents sick. We looked for danger, or at least what we perceived to be dangerous. We did whatever it took to survive and thrive, putting ourselves in harm's way. And we're better for it, even if some of us carry a few scars.

If we can learn from the past, and from today's less industrialized societies, then we will see that children require appropriate rites of passage to mark their transition to adulthood. Shopping at designer stores, surfing the Net for porn, successfully navigating the latest video-game adventure, and other such symbols of teenage acumen are not offering our kids the experiences they need.

There was a time when we, like most other cultures, prided ourselves on the rites of passage we offered our youth. A century and a half ago, young people apprenticed with their parents, assumed household responsibilities at an early age, attended community celebrations where there were people of all ages, and understood they had a place in their communities where they could make a contribution. It would be easy to romanticize such times, of course, forgetting that children were also removed from school at a young age, married off, or worse, indentured to employers. They were beaten and abused, and often saddled with too much responsibility.

So which story is more true? In fact, they are both true. One hundred and fifty years ago, during the dark days of Dickens's Industrial Revolution, and before the sanity of child protection laws, children needed protection and safety and didn't get it. It's a little-known fact that the first efforts to protect children from abuse in the United States began with Henry Bergh, who founded the Society for the Prevention of Cruelty to Animals (SPCA). In 1875, Bergh and his New York Society managed to protect eight-year-old Mary Ellen Wilson, who was being abused by her step-parents. Bergh rescued her by applying to the courts under the laws established to protect animals.[8]

And so it should be that children are protected from abuse and exploitation. More than a century later we have United Nations conventions signed by almost every country (the United States being an unfortunate exception), recognizing the rights of children. All this

can lead us to overlook that some children feel good about their contributions to their families when they take on roles such as working
instead of going to school. In the nineteenth century, as it still is
today in many countries, childhood ended sooner than necessary, but
it was an end that some children craved.

Many children, those with the most problems, tell me they want
something more than what their well-meaning parents have allowed.
Ironically, the adventure and responsibility they seek through jobs,
relationships, and physical challenges are often denied. In the black
hole of the middle class that tells children, "Hurry up and wait," a
small but significant percentage of our children are getting themselves into far worse trouble than they need to.

·2·

SUBSTITUTES FOR PROBLEMS

We are not doing our jobs as parents if we fail to prepare our children properly for life outside our homes. Young people, for example, especially summer students, are six times more likely than regular full-time workers to be injured or killed on the job.[9] Most often these deaths are youths who act recklessly at work or are untrained and therefore unable to protect themselves from the risks they face. In the first case, we have to ask ourselves if we've offered children enough coaching along the way for them to know how to take risks and keep safe in the process. It's much the same for those who are put in harm's way because of a lack of training. The young person who has never held a job until his early twenties is ill-prepared to know how to keep himself safe, how to ask for help, how to know when to say "No!" and risk being fired. Workplace tragedies are preventable. As parents, we can provide the framework to prepare our children for riskier situations when they are older.

Though overall our children are safer than at any other time in history, our overprotective ways as parents have created a host of other problems that signal a despondency, a disconnection between youth and their communities, with youth denied their responsibilities altogether. If working is dangerous, they are told not to work. That's all fine and good, except staying home with us prevents them acquiring the tools they need to grow up well.

And staying at home they are. Our children are marrying, on average, later than ever, as late as twenty-nine for men and twenty-seven for women.[10] And that means many of those Gen Xers are at home, still in their own rooms, with Mom and Dad doing their laundry and cooking their meals. It's our responsibility from the time they are little to help them embrace adventure and

> *We do our children no favours sheltering them from the challenges that come with living life fully.*

responsibility. We can do our jobs better. We can provide young people opportunities to experience risk and responsibility without returning to a time of exploitation, or allowing our children to exploit us.

I often surprise the audiences who attend my workshops by asking them, "At what age did you move out of your parents' homes?" In rooms full of parents, educators, social workers, and other mental health professionals, the majority report leaving home for the first time at seventeen, eighteen, or nineteen years of age. There is always a collective giggle in the room when we look around at ourselves. How could *we* have ever been competent enough at such a young age to make so many decisions for ourselves!

Some of us used our risk-taking behaviour as a strategic defence against overprotective parents. Others simply tumbled into danger because there was no one there to supervise us during tumultuous times. What was certain was that we all wanted to jump what Terri Moffitt, a New Zealand researcher, has referred to as the "maturity gap."[11] One way or the other, we were going to convince those around us we were every bit as competent as any adult.

And therein lies the problem. Just like us when we were kids, if denied opportunities to strut their stuff, our children will look to peers and gangs to experience loyalty and adventure; they will look to drugs to test their limits physically; they will look to sex to experiment with sensuality and attachments; they will seek jail time to prove themselves worthy of respect; they will steal to show they are clever; and they will bully to prove they are strong.

Do Something Different

While growing up, did you know any kids who were nothing but trouble at school or home? Who took endless risks and acted irresponsibly? Maybe you were that troubled kid. Recall all the ways that that child tormented his parents, teachers, and peers. The ways he drew attention to himself.

Now, extend him some compassion. For just a moment, try to understand him as he understands himself. That might be hard if your memories are full of anger and hurt. Maybe you were one of the troubled child's victims.

If even for a moment, though, you can step inside his shoes, what kind of world would you find? Would you find a confident child, or a child desperate for love and recognition? Maybe you'd find both. No matter who you find there, my guess is that you would find a child who had found a way to cope and feel powerful, despite the consequences.

The question we need to ask, though, is did that child really have any other choice?

Offer a troubled child a choice. Think about a child in your community who takes too many risks and endangers himself and others. Try the following:

- Say something nice to him.
- Let him know his unruly antics have caught your attention. Don't be mean, just be honest. Let him know if he's scared you, or made you worry for your own safety, or the safety of others.
- Let him know you are concerned for his welfare, not just yours.
- If you can, comment on something he is good at. All risk-takers are good at something, even if it involves danger.
- Somehow, convey to him he is still a part of your community. If he spends most of his time on the street, buy him a hot chocolate the next time you get yourself a takeout coffee. Offer him a drive (if you feel safe). Even just saying hello tells him he is someone important.

Each of these acknowledgements tells a troubled kid they don't need to act out to get noticed. It tells them they have a place in their communities. Who knows, if they feel like they belong, they may not need to endanger themselves or others in order to feel special.

THE 4DS OF PROBLEM BEHAVIOUR

There are children and youth whose only way to succeed has been through *dangerous, delinquent, deviant,* and *disordered* behaviours, the 4Ds of troubled kids. It is these behaviours that are, ironically, readily available to young people who are denied opportunities to experience the 4Cs, becoming *competent, caring contributors* to their *communities.* Throughout my career, first as a marriage and family therapist and social worker, then as a researcher and writer, children have told me over and over again that when there are no other ways to take risks that meet their need for something powerful to say about themselves, they will behave in ways that we adults label with one of those Ds.

Dangerous

Dangerous children threaten others, drive recklessly, jump from lake-side cliffs without checking the water below, experiment with fire setting, engage in unprotected sex, and seem bound and determined to conduct themselves in ways that show a careless disregard for their safety and the safety of others. These children exasperate us because they seem to stay stuck in these dangerous patterns. The two-year-old who climbs through the second-storey bedroom window and lands on the rosebushes below grows up to be the child admitted to hospital with an overdose, not because he is addicted to drugs, but because his curiosity got the better of him. To these children, life is always a series of challenges that present them with hundreds of novel ways to get themselves noticed. To parents, dangerous children are just one long series of accidents and trips to the emergency room. "Why can't they just calm down?" these parents ask themselves, then pick up the phone and call for help yet again.

Delinquent

Even more seriously, inside and outside jails I meet youth who fit the label of delinquent, whose behaviours are just as reckless and dangerous to themselves and others as the dangerous kids, but these children cross that line between lawful and unlawful. These are the children who steal cars for kicks, sell drugs for money, beat up others to feel powerful, and lie because it seems harmless. Today, aided by legislation that expands the definition of what a delinquent is, we are catching more children in our courts and jails than ever before but for crimes like drinking and driving, bullying, and carrying a weapon, crimes that would have gone unnoticed by the courts (but not our parents or communities) when we were children.

> *If we don't offer children experiences that make them feel more adult-like – like competent, caring contributors to their communities – then they will find their own ways.*

Deviant

Deviant kids are those who find their way to me because their families and communities are at their wits' end to know how to cope with their odd behaviour. At one time all a child had to do to be deviant was to declare himself a homosexual, not go to church, wear a strange haircut, or just hang out with the "wrong" crowd of kids. In general the deviant kid was one who didn't fit with the norms established by their families and communities. To their parents, teachers, and others in whose care they found themselves, their choices always seemed risky, threatening their moral and physical well-being. Times haven't changed very much. We still plead with kids like this to act more "normal," though our words are said in vain.

Disordered

Most serious of all are the disordered children, those who are victims as often as they are victimizers. They run away, then reappear inside our mental health institutions with foot-thick files documenting their strangely disturbed and frequently violent behaviours. They are seen as mentally ill and more likely to be excused for their excesses. They too take risks, only we think of those risks as symptoms of something wrong inside rather than any meaningful expression of who they are. Are we ever wrong! Conduct disorder and Attention Deficit Hyperactivity Disorder are the all-too common labels put on problem kids. These disorders are frequently used to explain the child's deviance, delinquency, and dangerousness. Children themselves will say that "going crazy" can be a tactic they use to excuse their love of risk. But this explanation goes all but unheard by parents and helping professionals alike. Sometimes, being disordered simply gives a child opportunities to do what the child really wants to do, like running away, doing drugs, being disruptive in class, not studying, or demanding attention when none is likely to be provided.

We need to offer children the right amount of risk and ways to express themselves that are robust substitutes for their otherwise dangerous, delinquent, deviant, and disordered choices – the 4Ds.

IT'S NOT JUST ABOUT RISK-TAKING

Of course, youths don't just seek danger. Jumping that "maturity gap" is also about behaving in ways that we associate with being adult. Risk-takers often want to appear more adult-like than they are. They think they can drive cars, stay out all night, and drink. Some do all three at once. Their behaviour may put themselves and others at risk, but their motivation is almost always to make their peers and parents look at them like they're already grown up.

Risk-takers, whether the adventure-seeking kind or those that take on too many responsibilities, are simply exploiting whatever opportunities they have to find something special to say about themselves. There's no sure way to know why a child chooses one set of challenges over another, though I will offer in the pages that follow some clues as to how we can *decode* what children are trying to tell us when they take risks, and how we can *communicate* better with our children so they hear us when we offer them substitutes that are less dangerous to themselves and others.

If we want our children to avoid problem behaviours, we need to offer them alternative risk-taking opportunities and responsibilities that we strategically provide. Even more, we need to back off and let them experience reasonable amounts of danger. When we don't, the results can be tragic.

Patrick has never had to worry about much. He has always been well-supervised. So much so that it was no wonder he adapted so easily to being in jail. The routine, the rules – neither has fazed him in the least.

He sits in front of me on a grey steel chair rubbing the marks on his wrists left from the handcuffs. He looks every bit the fourteen-year-old he is. His tousled jet-black hair needs a wash. Red pimples erupt across his chin. If he wasn't in the grey sweats the institution makes all young offenders wear, he'd look just like any other young man. He's not very talkative. With his drooping eyes and the way he looks everywhere but at my face, he's telling me I know nothing about what it means to be a young man in today's orderly world of endless expectations from parents. What would I know about boredom on a Saturday night or the tedium of six-hour school days that hold no promise? His records show that he wasn't measuring up very well to anyone's expectations. His grade eight report card tells me his life was Ds and maybe some Cs. Obviously, nobody had second-guessed themselves. Nobody had stopped to wonder what Patrick really wanted or what his options were if he couldn't be what others wanted him to be.

A year before we met, he had begun to shake the shackles of his bleak future by taking risks that he knew endangered himself and others. Big risks. He began stealing cars and taunting police. Now in jail, he says the "accident" he had caused a month earlier was just a mistake. A fifty-year-old father of three is dead. I know he didn't mean to kill the man. After a while you can tell which kids are lying and which are simply explaining their world to you in a way that makes sense to them. Patrick and some friends stole a car. When the police spotted them, they sped off and the game began.

Just weeks earlier, he had done the same thing. The police had stopped him only when they laid down a spike belt thirty kilometres up the highway from where they had first seen him in the stolen SUV. Remarkably, he'd been placed in the custody of his parents while waiting for a court date for that incident and nine others. It hadn't deterred him. He was confident enough to know that he could outrun the police every time because they would always call off the chase. They preferred to catch the kids later than risk them speeding down the highway, their hands on the controls of a three-ton weapon.

In our children's quest for danger, children can be either risk-takers, responsibility-seekers, or both. Adventure and danger, after all, come in many guises.

Patrick's parents couldn't understand their son. They didn't want him thrown in jail. They wanted him safely at home. They were certain after he'd been to court he'd settle down, get serious about his studies. They had long ago decided they'd protect him from the consequences of his actions. When Patrick had been kicked out of minor hockey for fighting and swearing, his parents had at first yelled at the coaches, then at Patrick. Eventually, exasperated, they'd shrugged their shoulders and told him, "You made your bed, now you lie in it," but they didn't mean it. They signed him up for soccer.

When Patrick began to drink on Saturday nights and would come home drunk, they took away his allowance and locked their liquor cabinet. They grounded him. Patrick didn't really seem to mind. Instead, he learned to steal money and pay adults to buy him alcohol. This won him the admiration of his friends.

When Patrick's school called and said he'd have to repeat grade eight, Patrick's parents yelled at the boy's teachers. They didn't know what to say to Patrick so they said little except he'd not have any television if next year his marks weren't better. It was Patrick's turn to shrug his shoulders. All his friends had digital cable. He'd hang out there and pretend to do his homework.

It never occurred to anyone that Patrick needed something other than the routines and discipline he was being provided. At the time, Patrick, like many children with similar patterns of behaviour, would likely have said he just wanted to have some fun. Getting to know him a bit better, I think he meant he wanted a challenge, something that he could succeed at doing that would bring him the same amount of attention he received for his problem behaviours. Something that would convince him, and others, he was someone important.

> Our children are telling us they need to experience some measure of risk in their lives. They need to feel the exhilaration of testing their limits.

Without a more conventional way to express himself, Patrick made the sensible decision to become the *best delinquent he could be*. It was a decision that was to turn his life, and the lives of others, into tragedies.

At first, Patrick wouldn't say much about the accident. He'd refused to admit to me that he was responsible for the death of the man. Eventually I asked him a question that was so different from any he'd been asked before, it changed our relationship. I leaned towards him and earnestly said, "So, what do you *like* about driving stolen cars?" Patrick now had something to talk about. Finally, someone had asked him the right question.

If someone had thought to ask Patrick that question a year earlier, the father of three might still be alive, and Patrick might be somewhere other than in jail. You see, Patrick could tell me what he liked about driving stolen cars. In fact, he became quite animated and sat up straight, enjoying the opportunity to explain to an adult how his friends see him as the most courageous kid they know. Even his time in jail only added to his stature among his peers. Besides, he liked the game of "catch me if you can" that he played with the police and the thrill of walking the line between total disaster and enviable success.

It would be easy to say that Patrick should have looked elsewhere for his thrills. But then, where? Who was offering Patrick anything else besides the bonds of control, conformity, and criticism? Nobody was offering him a substitute that had as much cachet as what he had found on his own.

While as parents we want to keep our children safe, the reasonableness of our actions makes no sense to our children. If we think back to our own childhoods, how many of us would have been content with being parented in the way we parent? How many of us wanted someone instead to open doors to excitement, wanted someone to provide us with the right kind of challenge, with the *right amount of risk*? Risk that we could cope with successfully. Risk that didn't overwhelm us but still made us feel like we were on the leading edge of all that we could be.

OUR FEAR OF CHILDREN'S RISK-TAKING

Instead we fear our children and their excesses. We worry *any* risk-taking will somehow lead to the kind of trouble Patrick has found himself in. In our exaggerated worry, we make our children's passions into problems that are more ours than theirs. Robert Epstein, former editor of *Psychology Today*, tells us that all this worry about teenaged angst is just one of a dizzying list of bad ideas generated by psychologists. "Teen turmoil, it turns out, is far from inevitable."[12] In fact, in many, many cultures, especially ones less industrialized, researchers have found no signs of teenagers needing to act in ways that separate them from their parents and communities. What do these others know that our culture doesn't? The answer could be as close as our own kids.

Too often, we give no thought to whether a child is ready and able to manage danger and responsibility. Worse, we overlook who is taking the most notice of our child and his or her success. It's that audience, as much as the adults in their lives, whom our children are trying to impress. The good news, though, is that our children actually want to impress us more than they do their friends. Surprisingly, even parents of juvenile offenders acknowledge that their kids are less influenced by their peers than they are by them![13] Our children's success still really depends on what we provide them with.

When we hold our children back, making our adult worries their problems, failing to properly assess the real risks they face from an over-abundance of security, ignoring their need to impress others and be accepted as someone special, we needlessly take risks away from our children. Seldom do we correct our mistake in time.

It's taken years for children to convince me that risk-taking – seeking adventure or responsibility – is a good thing for them to experience. In fact, I am now certain that the families with whom I have worked who have coped best with their children's risk-taking behaviours are those who offered their children *alternatives* that still provided lots of risk, but fewer consequences. Children in these families tell me they will give up their risk-taking behaviours that cause problems for themselves and others when we adults *offer the right substitutes*. These substitutes must bring with them recognition from adults and peers that the child is every bit as powerful and as (or more) widely accepted as he was while playing the bad kid.

But offering the right substitute is a challenge. If we are going to divert young people, we are going to have to offer them something just as intense, interesting, and powerfully evocative as they experienced through their dangerous, delinquent, deviant, and disordered behaviour. They are going to have to know that when they choose the substitute, they are still going to have people looking at them with the same awe and respect. It's a tall order to fill.

Do Something Different

Think hard.

Was there ever a time when you wanted to do something that would have endangered yourself or others, for which your parents found an adequate substitute? Maybe you weren't allowed to take a job working late shifts at the local gas station, but your parents were happy to help you buy the tools to start your own summer lawn-care business. Maybe you weren't allowed to date until you were sixteen, but were allowed to spend time at your cousin's cottage, where there were boys. Maybe you weren't allowed to go on your own to Europe for the summer at fifteen, but were allowed to visit your cousins in Florida without your parents tagging along.

Teenagers will generally accept a substitute if it brings with it some adventure and responsibility.

Start small. Think of one way you can offer your teen a little more risk, a little more responsibility:

- Extend your daughter's curfew.
- Let your son share a glass of wine at the dinner table.
- Let your son go to that rock concert after all, but arrange a time and place for pickup.
- Buy your daughter for her birthday one piece of clothing she really wants, and which you'd rather she not have. (A ripped pair of designer jeans? A studded collar? An undersized T-shirt?)
- Don't stand in the way of your teen taking a summer job out of town.

For some families, none of these tasks will be anything new. For other families, some of these tasks might seem far more serious than they were intended. Every family has its own rulebook. Trying something different means showing your child you are willing to reconsider the rules.

To paraphrase a well-known parable about a fisherman and a fish: *If we tell a child to stop doing something today, she will just find another, more dangerous and risky behaviour tomorrow. Offer a child a substitute to problem behaviour that is just as good or better, and that child will forever make better choices.*

It's no surprise that children who are overprotected answer back with more and more reckless behaviour. They storm out of our homes at midnight. They do drugs. They drive recklessly. They even choose to put themselves in jail. Sometimes they get pregnant. Sometimes, most tragic of all, they accidentally kill themselves.

Let's face it, like Patrick, at some point Tess, the four-year-old on the monkey bars I introduced in Chapter 1, is going to go looking for something powerful to say about herself. If she can't be the adventurer, the brave climber, the "in-your-face" *grrrl* who she was at age four, then what other choices will she have? Which peer group will offer the most powerful alternative? Judith Rich, in her award-winning work *The Nurture Assumption*, assures us that Tess's peers will be there at the ready to offer Tess these alternatives.

If not reckless self-endangerment, however, then what does a child do to make a big impression on others? What else can we offer a child Tess's age or a teenager like Patrick that will make them each feel just as self-confident as they tried to make themselves feel on their own?

Thankfully, children will change and leave behind problem behaviours when substitutes are provided.

•3•

THE RISK-TAKER'S ADVANTAGE

The immensely popular children's film *Finding Nemo* is all about a child's need to take risks. The film opens as Nemo's father is unable to prevent his wife and all his children, except Nemo, from being eaten. Not surprisingly, he has a lot of issues, not the least of which is he can't let his son grow up and become independent. Dad insists his little clownfish avoid taking risks at all costs. Still traumatized (can I really psycho-analyze a clownfish?), Dad is doing everything he can to make his life, and his son's life, predictably safe.

We all know where this is going, right? Nemo, off with some friends, swims into dangerous waters and is captured by a scuba diver who is collecting fish for his aquarium. It's now a race to see if Dad can save Nemo or if Nemo can save himself.

That's what makes the film interesting. Both Dad and Nemo share responsibility for surviving their ordeal. Each play a part, without which Nemo wouldn't be rescued. In typical Hollywood fashion, though, the film makes raising children fit neatly into a box. If only Dad had loosened up a bit in the first place and let his son play more unsupervised, then all this tragedy could have been avoided. If only it were so simple.

Yes, Nemo could have benefited from more exposure to manageable amounts of risk, but I'm not sure if he still wouldn't have pushed the envelope and insisted on doing things more dangerous than his dad, or any clownfish dad, would have let him do. Risk-taking is a game, and as adults we aren't always the ones setting the rules.

It's important we remember that risk-takers aren't necessarily deranged or out-of-control. Far from it. In many cases, when we understand what children are trying to accomplish through their risk-taking behaviours, we, their parents and caregivers, get clues as to how we can help them not only grow up and survive, but thrive amidst what Shakespeare called the "slings and arrows of outrageous fortune." With risk-taking comes the chance to share with others our unique identities. And surviving a particularly difficult challenge is just as likely to help us convince ourselves of our own self-worth as it is to make others take notice.

It works like this. Risk-takers are great at using their behaviours as a way to get *accepted* by whomever they admire. With risk-taking comes the possibility that others will recognize the risk-taker as someone special. When risk-takers find acceptance, they also find something *powerful to say about themselves.* Maybe it's "I'm the best skateboarder" or "I'm the best artist." Or maybe it's "I'm the best thief" or "I'm the biggest shit-disturber in my class." Either way, children who have gone out of their way to display their uniqueness are the ones seeking recognition from parents and peers, even if that recognition is for doing something bad. In the language of kids themselves, even a powerfully bad thing to say about one's self is better than having nothing to say at all. Hit a rough patch in life, and these same powerful ways of drawing attention to ourselves are likely to be used over and over again. Once a delinquent, I'm likely to stay the delinquent until I can be something else that is just as effective at making people notice me. It's the same for the athlete or the studious child. They are all searching for the same acceptance, only looking in different places, making use of whatever talents they have readily available.

I had heard some remarkable things about Mitch before I even met him. His mother said she was worried because he had failed grade eight and at fourteen had already run away four times. Each time, he'd stayed away a little longer and come home with bruises and cuts and the sunken eyes of someone who has been surviving on a steady diet of illegal substances. Perhaps, his mother thought, he was running away because he was afraid of a looming court date. Seems Mitch had been charged with kidnapping and confinement, as well as attempted assault. Later Mitch would explain to me it was just a prank. He and two other boys had captured another kid who he said was always bugging them. They'd tied him up in the basement of one of their homes, then threatened to slice his throat. "I was just there but had nothing to do with that part, the part with the knife," Mitch said. "That wasn't supposed to happen. We were just going to scare the kid, get him to leave us alone."

At first it seemed there wasn't much any of us could do to prevent Mitch from self-destructing. However, Mitch's mother also told me some fascinating things about her son, things I didn't expect to hear. She told me that *one* of the cars he owned had been ruined by some other kids, and he was going to get revenge. I stopped her.

"One of his cars?" I asked, checking my notes, ready to cross out fourteen next to "age" on the intake form and replace it with another higher number.

"Oh yeah, Mitch has always been good about saving his money. He's a good driver and bought both his cars all by himself, with his own money. He works on the weekends driving forklift for one of the shipping companies. His uncle is the foreman but works weekdays. He set Mitch up with the job."

"Where did he learn to drive?" I asked.

"His father taught him."

Her words were spoken so matter-of-factly that it was difficult to keep my jaw from dropping. The boy was hardly old enough to drive an electric scooter, much less a car, and yet here was a young fellow who was playing at being much older than he was. His behaviour, though, made some sense. Mitch's parents had separated eighteen months earlier when Mitch was twelve. He'd gone to live with his father at his downtown condo. A weekend alcoholic, Mitch's father all but denied Mitch access to his mother. Mitch didn't seem to mind. The house was quieter that way. The couple had been arguing and fighting for years. It was the same with Mitch, who had played his own part in the violence. His mother told me Mitch would hit her, just like her husband.

"He once had me up against a wall and choked me pretty hard when I made him study for an exam. He's never liked being told what to do."

Mitch's mother had moved back in with Mitch and his father a few months before I met her. Looking down at the floor to hide her moistening eyes, she told me, "That was the only way I could see Mitch."

It would have been easy to overlook Mitch's positive qualities. He was a violent kid, with a love for drugs and driving underage. And yet, oddly, he'd agreed to meet with me, not for his own sake, but to support his mother whom he felt sure was depressed. Sitting there with this young man who stood a full five feet eleven inches tall, I found myself somewhat confused by this complex individual. He could pass for sixteen, but showed the reasoning of a child. He had shown remarkable good sense when it came to making and spending money, but couldn't understand that fourteen-year-olds weren't supposed to drive, much less operate forklifts or abuse their mothers.

"Do you ever worry the police might catch you? Or that you might hurt someone really badly?" I asked him while we sat together in my office.

"I'm a good driver," he answered, stretching his long legs out in front. He ignored the second part of my question, about his violence, at least for now. "Besides, I make sure I drive safely, no crazy stuff that would tell the cops I'm an underage driver. That would be stupid." I agreed, and quickly wrote down what he'd said. Spending time with Mitch, I felt like Alice gone down a rabbit hole. Things weren't quite as they seemed.

Mitch's mother, of course, was worried. She wanted me to help her find Mitch a special school, one with a less structured curriculum. Her husband, when I spoke with him on the phone, thought Mitch would figure it out himself. His view was that his wife was coddling the boy too much. It wasn't likely, he figured, that Mitch would go to jail for one stupid prank. He'd come around, smarten up.

After all, Dad told me with some pride, Mitch was a smart kid. "He never even drinks and drives."

Mitch's life might look like a mess, but it proved remarkably easy to work with him and offer him some help. Once I started seeing Mitch the way he saw himself, solutions appeared. Mitch wanted to be respected as a young man, one who was already taking on responsibilities well beyond his years. Yet, when we spoke about how childish the violence, running away, and drug use made him seem, how much his behaviour made others question his maturity, Mitch paused to consider my words. He was much happier to be recognized as the responsible young man who held a job rather than the delinquent dropout. Trouble was, his mother was so concerned about his welfare, he had felt compelled to go to ridiculous lengths to convince her he could look after himself. Ironically, the more he acted alone, the more he convinced others how unprepared he was for life.

We may not always like our children's choices, but to change them and help them stay safe, we first have to tune in to what is motivating children to seek risk in the first place.

It was a start. Mitch kept his job and began to see school as a path to an even better job with better pay. We had lots of conversations about what he was capable of and how mature others thought he was when he was at work. We also talked about the role violence had played in making him seem childish, impulsive, someone who needed others to control him. It wasn't how he wanted to be seen.

Fortunately, Mitch had two paths he could follow into adulthood: one illegal and socially repugnant, the other more conventional. The last time I met him, things were looking much better. He went to court and was found guilty, but agreed to participate in community-based programming. He did everything the court told him to do. He even made and held to a commitment to stop his violence at home and with his peers.

Mitch also sold both his cars, deciding that he would rather save his money for a stereo and an iPod. Besides, he told me, he could still drive his dad's car now and again. He didn't need to have his own.

WHY RISKY BEHAVIOUR?

Our children, and we too, use our risk-taking behaviours to gain acceptance from others. How many of us take risks in the hope of impressing others? Sure, most of us do it in socially desirable ways. We interview for new jobs, go back to school in our thirties, drive our cars a bit too fast, or invest in the stock market. Maybe we dress a little oddly, or shave our heads. Heck, anything to stand out and make us feel unique and a little more important.

Our children are no different, but admittedly, have far fewer chances to experience danger or feel like adults. If Mitch, for example, hadn't been given a job at his uncle's warehouse, he wouldn't have had the opportunity to prove himself as a mature young man who could accept responsibility. In my experience, the more desperate a teenager like Mitch is to experience himself as being in control of his life, the more likely he is to get into trouble when socially acceptable opportunities aren't available.

Of course, our children's risk-taking behaviours have consequences not just for them, but for their parents and communities as well. Part of our responsibility to keep our children safe means providing them opportunities to grow. The better we get at offering them legitimate pathways into adulthood that include adventure and responsibility, the more likely they are to follow our lead. When we stop coaching children and let them carelessly take risks that really do allow them to endanger themselves, when we neglect to provide them with a safety net of the relationships they will need to help them pull their lives back together when they fail, then we are being negligent. It's our job to help children avoid taking risks they may be ill-prepared to take. At the same time, it's also our job to help them experience the risk they are ready for.

I've learned this as much at home as in my professional practice. I was out mountain biking with my twelve-year-old son, Scott, on trails maintained by a local mountain-biking club. Deep in the forest they had set up a series of catwalks made from cut branches and two-by-fours. The idea was to first jump your bike off the Big Whopper, a six-foot cliff, land without crashing into a tree conveniently growing in the middle of the path, then ride up a ladder of sticks, and over a series of levered bridges to the other side of a small river.

What nutcase, I thought to myself, designed such insanity? Though neither I nor my son attempted the course that day, other bikers did with some success. I watched my son itch to try the course too.

To Scott's credit, though, he thought better of it. At least for now. I know he'll eventually be up there on that catwalk. But I admire his common sense. We went farther down the path, and soon my son was jumping from three- and four-foot cliffs, slowly building up his confidence to try the Big Whopper. I figured it was a good compromise, though I'll admit each time he launched himself, my heart seized with panic.

WE NEED TO ENCOURAGE RISK-TAKING

In my experience, when properly encouraged and given lots of support, children who take calculated risks have an *advantage* in life over their more protected peers.

- Risk-takers are more likely to trust their own judgment
- Risk-takers have learned to respect the capacities of others and themselves
- Risk-takers know their limits
- Risk-takers understand the consequences of their actions
- Risk-takers (when grown up) are the ones who most readily reach out for help
- Risk-takers confidently assert their independence

No surprise, then, that risk-takers are both the pride of our communities when they succeed and our greatest challenge. There are days when we may well agree with the Marquis de Sade, who once said, "If a child shows himself to be incorrigible, he should be decently and quietly beheaded at the age of twelve, lest he grow to maturity, marry, and perpetuate his kind." Too cynical? W.C. Fields said it one better: "I like children. If they're properly cooked."

I say, better to understand what motivates risk-takers and help them achieve their goals, on their own terms. That may not be as funny, but it does create a more harmonious relationship with the young people in our lives.

Risk-taking isn't about being bad. It's about finding something to say about ourselves that makes us stand out.

How different it would have been for Tess, the four-year-old I introduced in Chapter 1, if her mother had asked her, "Do *you* feel safe up there?" as her daughter negotiated her way up the monkey bars. Mom could then have coached her daughter with gentle reminders to "Watch your hands and feet," "Pay attention to what you are doing," and most importantly, "If you need my help, shout." Their age may change, but our children need to hear these same messages whether they are four, fourteen, or even twenty-four.

Tess may have only been asking to climb a little higher on those turtle-shaped monkey bars. But in that moment of decision, what she heard was "Don't trust yourself," "Listen to others, they know better," and "You can't do what you think you can." All the fear and self-doubts of the parent came to rest on that little girl's shoulders. It was no surprise she so easily changed from the confident adventurer into the crying, dependent child.

Risk-takers beg us to let them push themselves to their limits. They do any number of things that put themselves in harm's way. The less destructive ones insist we let them go to the store and spend their allowance without a POS – that's kid computer talk for "parent over shoulder" – when they're still, to their parents' minds, too young to cross busy streets. Next we find them begging us to let them go to a dance, a rock concert, try a sport like rock-climbing, or join the air cadets. Just as often they want to help us fix the car or build the new back steps. They want to begin to use powertools and learn to cook. They want to have boyfriends and girlfriends. They want to drive dirtbikes. They want to go camping by themselves, stay out past their curfew, or get a tattoo.

In my work as a marriage and family therapist and researcher, each and every one of these requests has worried a parent at some time. Most parents eventually give in and let their children try new things, but many worry that their children are asking them to allow them to do things before they are really ready. But just as often I see families with children who have either heard "No, you can't" too often or whose need for adventure is so great that they recklessly endanger themselves.

There is no end to the ways children can find to live dangerously when they put their minds to it.

It has been ever thus.

Long ago a delightful story about a little girl in a red cape who goes to visit her grandmother in the forest was used to teach children about the dangers lurking in the real world. In the Brothers Grimm version of "Little Red Riding Hood," the story ends with the little girl being eaten by the bad old wolf, because that's what really can happen when we take responsibility for ourselves and aren't careful. Children loved it, no doubt because that's the way they see their world. They crave a good story that names their fears.

Later generations would have none of this. The Victorians were the first to sanitize the story by adding a woodcutter who kills the wolf and slits open its belly. Out pops Little Red Riding Hood and her grandmother, good as new. Nowadays we sugarcoat the story even further. In the Disney version, that bad old wolf doesn't even have a chance to gobble up what is rightly his.

I'm not sure our children are any safer, and their stories are certainly a whole lot more silly. We've missed the point. Children want to hear about risks and their own vulnerability. They want to know and feel the tremor of fear, even if only through story. Where has all the danger gone in our politely sanitized world?

Are we even certain that we want such a safe world? The psychologist Karen Pittman says, "Problem-free is not fully prepared."[14] It seems to me that most of us adults went out of our way while growing up to find that wolf, in one form or another. Many of us still do. At nineteen I drove a motorcycle as fast as I could and survived. I shudder even now to think how stupid I was. Most of my contemporaries, well-balanced, perfectly adjusted lower-middle-class kids, did exactly the same. I'm not sure I've entirely grown out of my risk-taking ways. Only now, before I do something really dangerous like visiting Israel and Palestine during wartime, or driving mountain roads at night in Northern Pakistan with broken headlights, snowboarding in the Rockies, or just living the daily drama of family life in the city, I check that my life insurance is paid up.

THE RESILIENT RISK-TAKERS

There is lots of evidence that risk-taking might be a good thing. There is a burgeoning literature on resilience and the predictors of healthy development when children grow up amid adversity. Resilience is a trait not just of individuals, but also their environments. Thriving despite the challenges life throws at us is about engaging with those around us to get what we need. It's not just about beating the odds; it's about changing the odds. That's why the children who survive best show a degree of plasticity,[15] an ability to adapt. But they also tell stories of fortuitous encounters that bring them what they need to grow up well.

Sadly, even children in relatively stable communities can experience the trauma of abuse, neglect, divorce, or the mental illness or addiction of a parent. Not to mention relocation between communities, and the regular challenges of failing grades, being bullied, or the death of someone close to them.

Children who survive these pitfalls best are also those who have the greatest number of developmental assets: individual, family, and community. Search Institute, a nonprofit organization in the United States, has named forty of these developmental assets, twenty internal, twenty external. Internal assets include things such as a commitment to learning and engagement in school, positive values such as responsibility and self-restraint, social competencies that include resistance skills that help young people avoid being pressured by others, and a positive identity with a sense of purpose. External assets are family and community supports, empowerment that comes from service to others, clear boundaries and expectations from adult role models, and the constructive use of time at home and in the community.[16] After interviewing more than 2 million youth, Peter Benson, Richard Lerner, and their colleagues have convincingly shown us that the greater the number of assets a child has, the more likely that child is to survive hardship.

What we need to ask ourselves, however, is what is the best way to acquire these assets? Does remaining protected and at no risk give children access to everything they need to grow up well? To me, the answer is an obvious "No!"

An international study that I lead has been trying to understand resilience across cultures and contexts. The International Resilience Project has identified fifty-eight common aspects of resilience among cultures as diverse as native peoples in North America, African-Americans, white suburban kids in Canada, orphaned children in Moscow, teenaged mothers in Tanzania, high-school students in Hong Kong, youth in countries at war such as Israel and Palestine, and those exposed to gang warfare and the threat of paramilitaries in Colombia and India. Remarkably, all these youth, boys and girls, identify a number of common aspects of their lives that help them survive and thrive. They say they need to:

- Feel a part of their local culture
- Feel like they have a say over their lives
- Feel like they can rely on others while at the same time exercising some independence and making their own choices
- Feel a part of their wider community
- Feel like they can contribute something to their communities through volunteer work, paid employment, or activities related to participation with a religious community
- Feel like they share responsibility for themselves and others
- Feel like they fit in somewhere, even while they feel unique in some ways among their family and peers
- Feel like they have ways to get their emotional and practical needs met

These are powerful needs and meeting them is going to mean taking some risks. In fact, in studies of adolescents who are more passive, who don't argue with authority figures, who never establish what is unique about themselves, there are higher rates of depression and even suicide.

Risk-takers, however, have an advantage. They find their resilience by pushing the envelope, placing themselves in dangerous situations that bring with them a sense of purpose, place, and passion. Should it surprise us that so many young people during wartime idealize joining the conflict?

The youth of today are every bit as capable as our veterans generations ago. And yet we offer them nothing to be so proud of.

My father-in-law, a gentle and kind man who spent his career as a university professor, continues to be fascinated by the history of the Second World War. He was too young to fight, but one can see among men of his generation the keen and unrealized desire to have been active participants in something that was so meaningful.

It is no different today. Unfortunately though, there are far fewer opportunities to feel a part of anything so noble. We have to look hard for those like Lieutenant-General Roméo Dallaire, who headed the UN peacekeeping mission to Rwanda during the horrendous 1994 massacre of more than 800,000 civilians. To hear Lieutenant-General Dallaire speak is to hear both the frustration and inspiration of the peacekeeper, to understand today just a little of the siren call our veterans must have heeded more than sixty years ago. Dallaire inspires us to place a "strategic focus on that higher plane called humanity" and warns us that "We are not allowed to abdicate that responsibility." These are heady words for youth to hear.

But we offer our children of the suburbs and safe small towns in the United States and Canada no such grandiose plan for their lives. We tell them to let others meet their needs, conform and stay in school, be like everyone else. We place no serious responsibilities upon them, invite them to take few risks, do not encourage them to hold jobs, and offer them few, if any, rites of passage on par with defending their country.

What are we thinking?

I have no desire to see young men and women go to war. But I am deeply moved by the spirit that mobilizes young people to take up such a cause. We must never forget this spirit. The risk-taker reminds us that he needs what his grandparents so tragically experienced through war. Our task as caregivers and parents is to find substitutes that are less lethal, but every bit as inspiring.

Do Something Different

Have you ever travelled to another community, either in your own country or another, where children are raised with very different expectations? If you live in the city, maybe you can recall time spent in a rural community where children are able to take more risks and expected to assume more responsibilities.

Wherever this other place is, think about your child living there. Would he do better than where he lives now? I often think that the child growing up in the suburbs, desperately bored and aching for adventure, would love time on a farm or in a remote logging community. There, he might find more socially acceptable ways to express himself. All-terrain vehicles and motorbikes, tractors and big barns, animals and open spaces all offer opportunities for a different kind of adventure than what city streets can provide.

If you can imagine your child enjoying his life more in a different community, you're closer to knowing what your child really needs. Finding sufficient risk and responsibility for an outgoing child is going to tax the resources of even the most creative parent. Thinking about this problem outside the box, by putting yourself in someone else's shoes, is a great way to identify options for a child who's looking for adventure.

Next time you have an opportunity to travel with your children, even if it is just a weekend family drive, think about where you can go to offer your child something different. Go back-country camping away from cars and modern conveniences. Splurge on an afternoon white-water rafting. Few suburban children can resist visiting a farm, no matter how much they protest along the way. Horseback riding, driving ATVs, and dirtbiking all provide children challenges that are beyond the typical.

Such activities give children new experiences of themselves and offer legitimate ways to experience some risk or responsibility. If you have more time, and are planning a vacation, consider the following:

- Don't go to Disney! There is no adventure there despite what the advertisements say. I'm not against amusement parks, but the child seeking risk and responsibility would do better on a ranch holiday in Colorado or Alberta than strapped into dizzying rides where the risk is nothing but illusion.
- Travel to another country. Get children their own passports and head overseas. This is a guaranteed way to provide children something powerful to say about themselves and an identity as a risk-taker that doesn't threaten anyone.
- Stay with a family you know in another part of the country where life is very different. Children who are asked to adapt to new cultures and ways of behaving most often rise to the challenge. What's more, they return home with a fresh perspective on what they can do and who they really are.

RESPONSIBILITY-SEEKERS

Not only have we made our communities too safe for our children's own good, we have also taken away opportunities for them to make a contribution. A decade ago prominent Israeli educator Raphi Amram took the microphone at a meeting of teachers of gifted children, children with mental and emotional disorders, and did the unthinkable. He asked not what we could do for them, but what *they could do for us.* "I have heard nothing about what gifted children should be expected to do for their society, about what they could be contributing with all of their gifts. I say this not just because society needs their talents but also because gifted children, like all children, need to hear such expectations for their own character development."[17]

Maybe we are making it too easy for our children to avoid responsibilities for themselves and others. Having taken away risk and consequences from their lives, what's left? Perpetual childhood? Languishing on our couches until work finds them? *Time* magazine recently introduced us to the "Twixters,"[18] that generation of very slowly maturing young adults in their late teens and early twenties who are staying at home, surfing a world of choices for careers, love, and lifestyles, just like they would a two-hundred-channel universe. Only, they're doing it on their parents' bill. Or they are toiling in low-paying jobs and having lots of fun, but still accepting little responsibility for their futures or the well-being of anyone but themselves.

Should we be surprised? What else have we demanded of them? Are these kids simply savouring the pleasures of irresponsibility that we have dished up, or is there a larger problem here? Has there been a breakdown of what *Time* referred to as the "cultural machinery used to turn kids into grownups"?

This phenomenon is being seen in many Western countries. In Canada they're called boomerang kids, the ones who return home. In England, Kippers, an acronym for Kids in Parents' Pockets Eroding Retirement Savings. We find them as well in France, Germany, Italy, and Japan. I've also, just to set the record straight, met them in Pakistan, Tanzania, Colombia, and China. Wherever a Western lifestyle has sanitized the lives of our children, children just seem to have decided it's too good a deal to give up living at home. Why bother with the hassle of actually doing something with your life when, frankly, you can have it all under your parents' roof?

Maybe that's why we need to heed Mel Levine's[19] advice and help kids make the transition to adulthood sooner rather than later. Levine, a professor of pediatrics and director of the University of North Carolina's Clinical Center for the Study of Development and Learning, is the author of *Ready or Not, Here Life Comes*. Levine says we need to build in children a sense of what it means to work, a sense of their future as something they create. He says we need to be careful that we don't make "childhood an impossible act to follow" with its wealth and security, but no responsibility. Finally, Levine encourages parents to help kids develop work skills, and to take on jobs so they understand how to work.

If all this makes sense to us as adults, it's not reflected in what we are actually demanding of our children. The result is that our children are becoming acclimatized to our excesses. I've been arguing that children need risk and responsibility: my greatest allies are the kids themselves. Many are begging for responsibility. Those that find both are the ones I worry about least. It is the Peter Pans, the ones who don't insist on growing up, who worry me. Will they ever achieve what their parents have achieved?

"NO!"

Responsibility-seekers, like their twins, the risk-takers, can act out in either conventional or unconventional ways. Both paths satisfy their search for a good challenge. I've met children who simply want the responsibility to paint their own rooms, make dinner once a week, order the Friday-night pizza, or look after a pet. More often than not, they're told "No!" or "Wait until you're older." Older children ask to drive their younger brother to his soccer game, stay at home by themselves overnight, use the shop tools, work at the mall, or set up a small business designing websites on the family's home computer. They want to get themselves up for school in the morning. See the doctor on their own. Choose their own church. Have their own money.

Again, all they hear is "No!"

We need to keep some perspective. I caught myself wondering at the validity of my own family's traditions after a recent visit with the Innu people of Northern Canada. A nomadic people, they were forcibly settled during the 1960s. Their homes changed from tents to wooden houses. There is a movement among the Innu to undo the effects of cultural genocide caused by forced resettlement, residential schools, and the ensuing pattern of disease and abuse. One of the most effective aspects of their cultural resurgence has been to reclaim their heritage as a nomadic people by offering their young people a chance to live back on the land, to hunt caribou and live in tents.

With that lifestyle comes many responsibilities. Children as young as ten work alongside their parents to prepare fresh kill. Children must also be able to handle knives and guns, drive snowmobiles, and know enough to keep themselves safe in a harsh Northern environment.

In contrast, on my children's tenth birthdays, each was given a Swiss Army knife with a two-inch blade. I know many parents who might think ten is still too young, but I chuckle when I think about my gift now and how much I underestimated my children's capacities. My children were ready far earlier than I ever imagined for more responsibility than I was willing to give. I need only look to my Northern neighbours to understand all that children are capable of doing.

Too often, when we fail to provide opportunities to feel more adult-like, our children find their own. Not all the strategies they employ will be as extreme as those used by Mitch. Sometimes what teens do is quite innocent, though their actions still carry consequences and spark conflict with parents. Fifteen-year-old Marion used smoking as one way of proving she was old enough to make her own decisions. As Marion explained to me, "My mom makes such a big deal out of my smoking." She rolled her big dark eyes, then stared at me from beneath bangs of jet-black hair cut with razor-sharp precision. She couldn't smoke in my office, so she let her hands wander to her mouth, nibbled at her fingernails. "It bugs me, really, but I guess she knows what it can do and all that," she said with a sigh, distracted by a painting on my wall of Masai warriors I'd brought back from Tanzania. Like the Innu, the Masai understand what it means to provide their youth with rites of passage appropriate to their age. Marion might as well have been living on a different planet, her experience growing up was so different.

"Life isn't such a big deal," Marion insisted. "Like I could see my mom saying 'no' if I was doing drugs or walking down the road with a beer in my hand and I could get hit by a car, then I'd understand. But smoking's not going to kill me, at least not in the short term."

Marion could make lots of distinctions between appropriate and inappropriate behaviour. She understood what it means to act responsibly. She knew enough to limit her consumption of drugs and alcohol. However, when it comes to smoking cigarettes, the boundary line between what's acceptable to her and not acceptable to her mother was quite different. It was as if she had decided that smoking was a part of how she saw herself, though on other issues she walked in step with the values of those who had raised her.

"What does it say about you, the smoking?" I asked, trying to open space for Marion to think about this from her mother's point of view. "Your mom thinks it says a lot about you and who you are."

"I think I'm exactly the same person whether I smoke or not," Marion said with a snort. "I don't think about it much. It doesn't seem like a big deal to me." Her mother, a reformed smoker herself, thought it was an incredibly irresponsible thing for her daughter to do. The hypocrisy hadn't been lost on Marion, who insisted, "I can quit anytime. *Like my mother.*"

In my work with young people, I have tried to discover what motivates them to do things that are potentially self-destructive. Like smoking. What are they looking for? And why can't they find these things in socially acceptable ways? It's often exactly the same thing we adults went searching for at their age. Marion's mother, after all, had once been very much like her daughter. If we were going to get Marion to stop smoking, we'd have to get Marion's mother to remember her life as a teenager and what smoking meant to her. Not surprisingly, when the two of them began to speak about the *good* things that smoking does for teens, slowly they were able to share ideas about alternatives that might have been as good for Marion's mother as they could be for Marion now.

Let's face it, smoking by itself means very little. It's the cachet that comes with smoking that makes it worthwhile. It's the message that one sends that tells others, "I'm old enough to control my own body," and "I'm responsible for my own decisions." These are the real perks to inhaling, no matter what the health risks.

HABITS AND THE IDENTITIES THAT FOLLOW

Unfortunately, understanding the benefits a child gets from acting out may not dissuade her from a self-destructive habit. It's a tough sell for any parent to argue against the combined forces of marketers and addiction. And the marketers are clever. They have recognized this same search for power by our children that I have been describing.

Continuing our tobacco example, strategies by governments, in partnership with the tobacco industry, to create zones around schools where anyone under the age of twenty-five must show identification to purchase tobacco products, has been the best advertising for the tobacco industry cigarette producers could have bought. And we dutifully applauded tobacco companies as good corporate citizens who encouraged our children to act responsibly.

Accepting children's identities means valuing them for who they are. These identities are their way of defining themselves as powerful, responsible young people. Parents need to acknowledge children's search for personal responsibility even if they don't accept how they express it.

What we forgot to do was think about the problem of tobacco use from the perspective of the kids. By restricting tobacco use to those over a certain age, and enforcing it as one would any other legally restricted activity (like driving a car, voting, and the consumption of alcohol), the message was conveyed to our children that smoking is an adult activity. The marketers, however, understood that the trick was to see the world as kids see it. They want to be seen as independent and adult. If instead, we offer children another, equally powerful way to jump the maturity gap between being a teen and being a responsible adult, they will be more likely to follow our lead and put out their cigarettes.

Many parents tell me their children push them to give them more responsibility than they are ready to give. They need to remember that what is not given will be taken. Responsibility-seekers with few opportunities to test their limits can always look outside their families for permission to care for others and ways to feel older. Children's peer groups offer them lots of possibilities. Our children can help other children steal. They can help classmates cheat. They can be the leader of a gang, even if the gang they lead is just a bunch of kids who go for a smoke off school property. They deal drugs to get money. They become sexually active to assert their control over their bodies. They even do things as outlandish as steal a car so they can drive their friends home from a party, our children's own interpretation of what it means to be the designated (and therefore, responsible) driver. Responsibility-seekers do many of the same things as risk-takers, but not for the adventure. They're out there to convince everyone they can look after themselves.

What is a risk to a child will depend on the child's perception of the world.

The children with whom I have worked have told me that these problem behaviours are very often their ways of finding opportunities to experience the responsibility they need to convince themselves they are adults-in-the-making. William Damon, a Stanford University psychologist, made the same point in 1995 in his book *Greater Expectations*. Damon reminds us that personal responsibility and high standards do have a place in children's lives. By expecting more of our children, we do ourselves and them a favour.

THE DIFFERENCE BETWEEN RISK AND DANGER

The trouble with understanding a child's risk-taking and responsibility-seeking behaviour is that *risk* and *danger* mean different things to different people. Every culture sets rather arbitrary limits on what is and is not a risk to its children and what is perceived as dangerous.

Risk is different from danger. Risk is about the perception that something bad *might* happen as a result of seeking adventure or responsibility. It's a best-guess scenario, sometimes based on science, more often based on some combination of common sense and the wisdom handed down to us from our parents.

Danger is more *immediate* than risk. There is less guesswork. Even a child knows when danger is present. Many children in fact go looking for it intentionally.

When children and their parents argue, it is most often about whether risk really exists. This is a question of *perception*, and not surprisingly, teenagers and adults frequently disagree. In cases where both generations do agree, their next argument tends to focus on the specific dangers the risk poses. Inevitably, this becomes a question of *competence*. Does the teenager have the capacity to cope with the danger the risky situation poses?

Take for example an unsupervised house party your fourteen-year-old wants to attend on a Saturday night. Of course, there are lots of potential risks, and a mature teen will acknowledge that, yes, there is the likelihood that some older teens might sneak in alcohol, some teens might experiment sexually, and that the

We are likely to agree with our children about what is and is not dangerous but disagree with them about their capacity to handle that danger.

house where the party is being held could be damaged. The risk-taker will insist on attending because the party promises excitement and danger. "You never let me have any fun!" he shouts as he refuses to listen to you and storms out of the house. The responsibility-seeker will demand she be allowed to attend the party to prove she is adult enough to handle these dangers. "Don't you trust me?" she shouts as she slams her bedroom door after being told "No! You can't go!"

In both cases, the teens are very clear what it is they are looking for. The risk-taker wants "fun," the responsibility-seeker, "trust."

When parents respond with a promise to find an equally compelling way for youth to get their needs met, they are much more likely to avoid family conflict and tears. After all, there are other things fourteen-year-olds can do. There is the grade eight dance and the curfew extension they'll need to attend it. They can take the bus across town for an afternoon at the mall with three friends or travel on their own halfway across the country to stay with a friend who moved away. They could even go to a rock concert where there will be at least some supervision.

Many of the things our children ask permission to do are things they would argue pose a manageable amount of risk. David Ropeik and George Gray, co-authors of *Risk: A Practical Guide for Deciding What's Really Safe and What's Really Dangerous in the World Around You*,[20] tell us that risk is half fact, half perception. How we feel about a risk, to ourselves or our children, our affect and intuition, is going to be the determining factor when we size up whether a particular risk is manageable. "Different risks mean different things to different people."

Our children are constantly having to convince us their worlds are less risky than we think and their capacities to handle danger greater than we give them credit for.

Like adventure-seeking, responsibility can also bring our children a *perception* that they are taking a risk and in the process help them feel more adult. It's two sides of the same coin. Think back. When were you first allowed to stay at home by yourself? When were you ready to have a more serious relationship with a member of the opposite sex? What about your first job or other extra-curricular activities? How much convincing did it take to get your parents to agree that you were ready for the responsibility that came with working the late shift at McDonald's, or balancing schoolwork with playing on the regional basketball team? Each of these activities exposes children, physically, emotionally, and academically, exposure they need to mature.

FOUR POWERFUL MESSAGES

Growing up, most of us pushed ourselves, and as a result of the risks we took, we not only survived, but *thrived*. Risk-taking and responsibility-seeking are behaviours coveted by children because both bring with them the chance the child will hear four powerful messages from both adults and peers. These four messages are:

- *"You Belong"*: Children need to know they fit in somewhere, and that they are loved by those around them.
- *"You're Trustworthy"*: Children flourish when they know "Others trust me" and "I can trust myself."
- *"You're Responsible"*: Children want to hear that they are seen as adults, or at least soon-to-be adults. They want to be responsible for their own lives and share responsibility for the lives of others.
- *"You're Capable"*: Children grow up best when they know they

have special talents and are able to make good decisions for themselves, both important to feeling capable.

It doesn't matter to our children whether they get to hear these messages by being risk-takers or responsibility-seekers. Children tell me
they find ways to hear these messages by being either good, or when
that fails, by being bad. At least, that's how we adults see their behaviour. Good behaviour is behaviour we approve of. Bad behaviour is
always something devilish, something that breaks our rules.

OPPORTUNITIES FOR GROWTH?

Children are far more utilitarian than adults. They'll behave in whatever way they have to in order to survive and thrive. If reckless self-
endangerment gets them more praise from peers than being a "goody
two-shoes," then so be it. If they have to get pregnant to have any
hope of being treated like an adult, then that's typically fine by them
as well.

Obviously, I would prefer children hear these four messages from
adults and peers who are recognizing them for socially acceptable
behaviours. Children say the same. They would rather be noticed by
parents and peers for taking well-managed risks than for acts of self-
destruction and the thoughtless endangerment of others.

But the choice is not always theirs. The *opportunities* children
find to express their passions depend on the restrictions parents,
schools, and their wider communities place on them. Depending on
how flexible parents are, and how rich with opportunity their environments, children will make the best of what they have.

Children, after all, are eternal optimists. Like the small boy in the
Broadway musical *Les Misérables* who sings, "The world is big but
little people turn it around," our children never give up in their quest
to have someone notice them. Risk-taking behaviours and demands
for more responsibility are simply their best strategies to get noticed.
Were we any different when we were growing up?

Likely not. I'm often surprised, in fact, by the expectations of
parents who are recent immigrants from war-torn countries. A mother

and father with whom I worked had managed to escape Serbia. They knew everything there was to know about taking risks. They'd had to put their lives on the line many times. Strangely, that same spirit was something they demanded their children ignore. Their daughter, Vicki, was trying hard to fulfill her parents' expectations. She studied hard, played the piano, stayed at home like she was supposed to. Yet, her life was quickly crumbling. She developed anorexia, starving herself slowly. It was a reasonable solution. Indeed, her body was just about the only part of her life she had any say over. Not eating was a simple way to expose herself to some danger and responsibility.

As her weight dropped, she also got noticed. And not just because thin is in. Her weight loss got her referred by her school guidance counsellor to an eating disorders clinic. There, with support from a family counsellor, Vicki won some concessions from her parents. She could stop playing piano, have a few more friends, and be a good, rather than exceptional, student. It was a difficult transition for her parents. Still afraid that what they had achieved would be taken away, they had trouble accepting that their daughter didn't experience life with the same panic. Vicki knew nothing of their fear of failure. Fitting in, being an average kid, was enough. It was also the solution to her eating disorder.

RISK-TAKERS AND RESPONSIBILITY-SEEKERS HAVE POWERFUL IDENTITIES

If our children are lucky, they'll convince themselves and others they are a person who belongs, is trustworthy, responsible, and capable. They'll hear the four messages and with them achieve one *powerful identity*.

Notice, however, that I'm not talking about identity as something that we engineer deep inside ourselves. Our identities are forged from our relationships. We know who we are when we perform for others and are rewarded with recognition for that performance.

The risk-taker, whether putting himself in danger, or taking on too much responsibility, is performing elaborate choreography. He is inviting others to *mirror* back to him something special about himself. He is asking the adults and peers in his audience to notice him.

In this dance of push and pull, the child is trying to control how others see him. Risk-taking is, to state the obvious, the easiest way to influence how others see us. The children I meet with who have powerful identities, identities that impress others for one reason or another (good or bad), are the ones who tell me they know how to use their risk-taking behaviours to impress others.

We develop an identity when we perform for others, convincing them we are special and unique. Children seek to control how others see them, usually by choosing to perform in ways that will make others see them as powerful and worthy of their respect.

I can't blame children for being overzealous. They start their race for respectability in the outside lane, disadvantaged from the time the starter's pistol sounds, for we just don't want to admit that children are more capable than we make them out to be. We look at them as less evolved beings, as if somehow their personal development mirrors the development of our species, from savage primate to a more cultured, sensitive human. As the Norwegian children's researcher Jens Qvortrup warns us, we are stuck with our view of our children as "human becomings" rather than "human beings." And it's only human beings who are competent, special, responsible, and respected. What choice do our children have but to go mad, act bad, or feel sad? If we don't cut them more slack, open up more space for our kids to experience the adventure and responsibility they crave, they are going to act like unruly prehistoric hominoids just to throw our prejudices back in our face. "There," they'll say. "Now live with that!"

Though our children show great promise, we are failing miserably at preparing them for the day they will be asked to give back more than they take. We need to let them practise tackling danger and being responsible *in manageable ways*. If the overprotective parent is denying his children the opportunity to grow, then the under-supervising parent is burdening her child with the disadvantages of neglect. Too often, we are either throwing at children more risk than they can handle, more responsibility than they want, or not enough of both. We have to strike a better balance if we truly want our children to be safe.

Overprotected children are begging us to offer them some benign neglect, a little space to figure the world out on their own. They need the chance to be free-range kids once again, to take risks that are unscheduled, without uniforms, and beyond the control of their parents. Their under-supervised peers have different needs. They shout, "Would someone please give a damn!"

For all our sakes, we had better start listening.

WHATEVER HAPPENED TO CHILDREN'S RITES OF PASSAGE?

In our mania to keep our children safe we've forgotten that children not only need the opportunity to test their limits, and learn from us how to manage the risks they face, they also badly need *rites of passage*. They need experiences that mark their transition from being children to adults. How many of us can remember such moments? Perhaps it was the time our parents left us overnight alone; maybe it was when they let us buy our first car. Or perhaps it was a transition made out of necessity: a parent became ill, or pregnant, and we were cast into the role of chief cook and bottle-washer, breadwinner, household mechanic, chauffeur, or confidante. In my experience, rites of passage signal to the child, "You're practically there, kid."

Instead of "hurry up and wait," children need to know when it's time to grow up. The best rites of passage combine elements of both risk-taking and responsibility-seeking. Generations ago, and even today in many cultures around the world, children would go through elaborate rites of passage to prove themselves. They would be exposed to great amounts of danger, all so that they could assert, "I am now an adult." In Tanzania, I've met thirteen-year-old Masai boys who spend months in small groups on their own surviving off the barren landscape of the Serengeti until they are ready to rejoin their tribe. In Colombia, girls as young as eleven are put to work selling food on the streets, proud of the contribution they are making to their family's income. Closer to home, my neighbour's fifteen-year-old son operates a chainsaw for a small logging company on weekends to make money. My colleague's fifteen-year-old daughter spent a year in Sweden as part of an international youth exchange.

It's time we reconsidered what our children are capable of doing. We need to tell them how much we trust them and show respect for their choices so that they will trust us when we do give them some good advice.

DANGEROUS BY NATURE?

The parents of my daughter's rambunctious friend are quick to tell everyone, "She popped out a strong-willed child and hasn't changed since." That could explain a lot. Jaiping is one of those rough-and-tumble children who are forever falling out of windows, breaking bones, and causing mayhem. I'm glad my daughter has chosen her as a friend.

Is our children's love of risk-taking behaviour something that is in their *nature,* or is it something we *nurture,* the consequence of traumatic experiences, or the bad luck of being born in families that ignore them? Why do some children who are looking for risk prefer recklessness, while others prefer the challenge of assuming adult responsibilities?

There are no clear answers to these questions. And such abstract musings do little to help us know what to say to a thirteen-year-old who has just been caught drinking behind the mall with boys two years older than her. There just isn't a perfect solution, or some magic gene therapy, that will put good sense into our children's heads. But we can think about our children's lives as they experience them. We can ask ourselves if that thirteen-year-old has any other equally exciting way to convince herself she is older, more mature, and ready to be taken seriously as a young woman. In my experience, most teenaged girls aren't looking to put themselves in danger. But they do enjoy the recognition that comes from knowing they can turn heads and be taken seriously. It is not a cop-out to say there is no cookie-cutter solution to such behaviour. The best strategy is to offer a substitute, one that brings with it just as much notice and power. To my reasoning, any kid who has already made her way to behind the mall is already too hungry for risk and responsibility to listen to her parents when they tell her to come home and be a kid.

Instead, we are going to have to work with what we have and mould our children over time into adults who are ready to assume both the rights and privileges we enjoy as their parents. For many of the families I've met, helping their children find paid or volunteer work, giving them a little more responsibility, and easing up on some rules is often a beginning to saving children from the street. I encourage limits on any behaviour that is life threatening or morally threatening, but I'm also quick to encourage families to allow children opportunities to look after things that are more their concern than their parents'. After all, no one gets hurt if a teenager dresses funny, paints her room black, or chooses her own friends. Far better than the other options: early sexual activity, eating disorders, running away, suicide, or truancy.

> *Our role as parents is not to limit opportunities for our children, but to help our children thrive amidst danger and embrace risk in ways that will ensure their long-term immunity to self-destruction.*

When parents work with children's tendencies to take risks and seek responsibility, they are more likely to succeed. That is the risk-taker's advantage. Vicki might trouble us with her behaviour, but at least she had the compulsion to go looking for what she needs. The risk-taker is simply that much more likely to hear the four messages that are the cornerstones of a healthy individual: you belong, you're trustworthy, you're responsible, and you're capable.

•4•

OVERPROTECTED OR
UNDER-SUPERVISED

While Vicki in the last chapter deals with *overprotective* parents, there are just as many children in my middle-class community whose lives are marred by a lack of supervision. These are the children thrust out into the world without the support they'll need to make it. They may be "fortunate enough" to be driven around in the latest model suv. They may have the latest version of interactive video game on their own television in their own bedrooms. And their homes may be so large that each child has his or her own bathroom. But they are not supervised. There are no adults really watching them. It's not surprising, then, that when trouble happens, parents of these children are the ones most blindsided, their embarrassment at meeting their children in jail or in the drug rehab centre, unimaginable. Even their child having to do summer school comes as a complete surprise. *Under-supervised* children are just as likely as their overprotected peers to drift into risk-taking and responsibility-seeking behaviour that brings them more problems than they are ready to handle.

These patterns to parenting bring with them consequences that affect children from the time they are very young. It's these early experiences, I've learned, that exert a dramatic influence on the behaviour of our teenagers.

If Tess's mother, whom I described in the first chapter, was over-protective of her daughter, the little boy with glasses sitting alone on the swing next to my daughter appears to be unsupervised. He's only five years old, but already there is no adult any longer anticipating his needs. I watch him for a few minutes trying to make his swing move. His little legs pump forward and back like he's seen older children do, but he gets nowhere. No one seems to notice, though. Even more surprising, he calls no one for a push. He just keeps trying all on his own.

In a world ruled by fear and shame, we think of everyone as either victims or perpetrators, and our children as individual responsibilities.

I can only stand the suspense for so long, and after a few minutes I turn and ask him, "Would you like some help?" He nods, and I give a few gentle pushes, all the while scanning the park for his mother or father. A ways off, a man sits with a newspaper and a cellphone. He's heavy-set, with dark black hair. He's got a cooler beside him. The second time I push the boy, I see the man look up and stare over the top of his paper, then go back to reading. Dad, most likely. I decide to wave, but he's buried behind his paper before I can raise my hand. The little boy whose name I never know says a polite, quiet "Thank you" and happily continues to pump his little legs back and forth.

I'll admit, like many parents today, I'm always anxious about helping a child who isn't mine in public places. I'm always worried about what parents will think. What will they make of a strange man touching their child even if it is only in the most innocent of ways? I hear other parents say they too are no longer willing to take responsibility for the unsupervised children in our communities. We have all become too burdened with the fear that our small acts of kindness will be misunderstood or be taken as a slight against how other parents parent.

It's our children who lose out. What does that little boy have to do to get an adult to notice him? What risks will he one day take to convince his parents he needs their attention? Looking at him, with his sandy blond hair and dimpled smile, he reminded me of a boy I once worked with who had discovered that the youth workers at the jail where he was sentenced were more concerned for his well-being than his own parents. At least at the jail, Darren told me, someone knew he was alive. His parents provided for him whatever he needed materially but were emotionally absent. The third time Darren was caught stealing car radios, he hadn't even tried to hide what he was doing. He knew he was being watched. Far better, he reasoned, to be in jail and have a powerful identity as a thief than to exist invisibly as a neg-

When we hold our children back from taking chances, we force them to seek out more and more dangerous ways to say something special about themselves.

lected child with few prospects to succeed, academically or socially. The youth workers were like well-polished mirrors. When Darren looked into their eyes, he enjoyed what he saw: recognition that he wasn't a bad kid, but a kid who lacked attention and love. They could see past his delinquency, but were powerless to offer him much more than a period of respite from the emptiness he experienced back home.

Being the polite little boy on the swing may evoke help from concerned others, but it's not getting him what he will really need to thrive. Maybe, just maybe, he will figure out one day that if he really kicks up a fuss, screams, and terrorizes others, then his father will *have to* put down his newspaper.

OVERPROTECTIVE OR UNDER-SUPERVISING: WHICH ARE YOU?

Nature, nurture, overprotected, under-supervised? How do we help our kids when it all seems so confusing? I'd like to say it's simple, but it isn't. There are lots of moving targets here, and trying to hit the mark with the right parenting style that will keep the risk-taking child safe is not a perfect science. But there are some things we can do that are more likely to help.

First, let's start with you as a parent. Later we'll look at the kids and the risks they face, but it all begins with us and what we are comfortable allowing our children to do.

Think about your role as a parent (or caregiver like foster parent, teacher, grandparent, group home worker, Big Sister), and how you relate to the children in your care. If we think of the child's need to take physical and emotional risks, then how do we respond?

Physical risk-taking

Consider how you are teaching your child to take physical risks. Does the child have responsibility for his own body? If the child is more quiet, less willing to take risks, do you offer activities like climbing gyms, Outward Bound–like adventures, or the rough-and-tumble of mastering a martial art? If the youth is already very outgoing, do you find increasingly challenging opportunities for him to be physically active: sports teams, mountain biking, whitewater rafting, hiking the Rockies?

In my own children's case, they were spending so much time on the monkey bars in the park or doing chin-ups from the doorframes that I decided to install a set of bars in a main floor hallway using old car racks and some recycled pipe I found in someone's trash. Many an amused parent, when they see these exercise bars suspended above them in the entranceway to our home, have asked me if those are what they think they are. My children and their friends are only too happy to show off and literally climb the walls of my house demonstrating what they can do. Rarely has a boy or girl entered our home and not given them a try, straining to do at least one chin-up or happily swinging hand over hand from one end of the hallway to the other.

The strategy was not entirely frivolous. Installing the bars created a sense of danger and excitement right there in our own home. It's a little like having our own gym. It also gives my children status among their peers. My children don't have the latest video games or even cable television, a serious setback for most teens. But somehow their friends still flock to our house to swing from the ceiling or join in mammoth games of capture the flag in the vacant lot behind us. We make the most of what we have, inside or outside our home.

Emotional risk-taking

If we are reluctant to allow our children to take physical risks, then we are even worse at allowing them to bruise themselves emotionally. When they're small, do we allow them to choose their own friends? Even when they risk rejection or befriend a bully? Do we let them suffer the consequences of being rude (by making them undo the damage they cause when they hurt others' feelings)? Do we let them wear the wrong clothes and suffer the embarrassment? Do we let them experience the disappointment of spending their money on a toy we know they won't like but insist on buying (hopefully they are spending their own money, saved from allowances or birthday presents from grandparents)? Do we insist they sometimes push themselves emotionally, forcing them to phone their grandparents and say thank you for those birthday gifts?

Risks need to be managed, not suppressed.

In their teen years they will face similar emotional risks in their relationships with their peers. Will we let them experience first love? What about first rejection? Will we let them again choose friends, be rude to us, then insist they find ways to make amends? Will we encourage them to volunteer or stand up in their communities for something they believe in, and encourage them to think for themselves?

HOW DO WE HANDLE OUR CHILDREN'S RISK-TAKING?

The challenge is to offer children the right amount of risk in raising them to be well-prepared adults. There are a lot of things to consider when deciding how much to supervise children, what kinds of risk to expose them to, and what responsibilities they are ready to handle. No wonder many parents slide to one end or the other of the scale and are either overprotective or under-supervising. It may be easier to find one pattern of parenting and stick to it no matter if it is appropriate or not, but it does our children no good.

One of the more appropriate ways to parent in *most* situations has been well charted by parenting guru and educator Barbara Coloroso. For years, she has spoken about the advantages of "back-bone" parenting. Coloroso's backbone families provide their children with structure and the flexibility to negotiate for what they need as they grow up and become ready to take responsibility for their own decisions. In contrast, "jellyfish" parents let their kids roll over them, with the kids the losers in the process. "Brickwall" families make their children mind them on every rule, never teaching children to think for themselves.

What Coloroso doesn't explore, however, is what happens when the context in which we are raising children changes. It's then that a more ecological model of parenting is needed, one that is capable of responding to the world as it shifts. For example, African-American single parents raising children in high-risk neighbourhoods in Philadelphia showed researchers that the most brickwall among them had the most successful children. These were women, mostly, who told their children what to do because the dangers those children faced just getting to and from school were so great it was beyond their capacity to keep themselves safe on their own. In this case, however, there was very real danger. The kids knew they had to listen to their parents if they were going to stay in school and have a future that was less than bleak.

The challenge for families living in more secure communities is that they can mistakenly assume from the media hype that their communities are crime-ridden danger zones. Risk doesn't treat us all as equals. In fact, in studies of risk exposure, it has been shown that only a very few people in a community will experience most of the bad things that happen. In the average small city, this means that the acts of violence and theft that people read about daily are most likely occurring to only a few people.

And yet, we often respond with brickwall tendencies when our children rightfully ask for more access to risk and responsibility to prove themselves more mature. We misread the signs. Our rules become out of step with our children's perceptions of the dangers they face. When children lose confidence in our ability to distinguish between media hype and real danger, they are not likely to heed our advice, nor obey our rules.

It's as if we have come to see our children as "defective adults," as author Evelyn Waugh once quipped. I prefer instead to see what neuropsychiatrist Bruce Perry sees: "Malleable" children who when exposed to trauma adapt with a variety of different responses. Some fight, some take flight.[21] Perry has a bias towards the kids who fight. The child who surrenders, who gives up and behaves as the dutiful child, ever obeying his parents, taking no action to resist

> *A child who must resist the overprotective ways of caregivers in order to grow is also a child who is beyond the influence of caring adults who might have wisdom to offer in times of crisis.*

those who hurt him, is the child more at risk for problems later in life. Perry says, "A piece of the child is lost forever." That compliant child loses something developmentally. Their brain quite literally doesn't grow in the way the more resistant child's brain grows. It's the more outlandish youth who is likely to experience emotional, behavioral, and cognitive development after trauma. According to Perry, their behaviour helps them to realize their potential. The evidence is all there. There is no advantage to keeping our children's lives too safe, expecting of them nothing but compliance with our rules.

PROBLEM PARENTING

Here's just a short list of some of the ways overprotective and under-supervising parents relate to their risk-taking children.

The Overprotective Parent
- They say "No!" more than they say "Yes!"
- They are unwilling, or unable, to coach their child through risky behaviours, fearful of the child getting hurt.
- They tell their child all the bad things that *could* happen, but ignore the child when he tells them all the good things he *wants* to have happen.

- They look at the world through the lens of their own past experience with danger.
- They put their child's safety above their child's need for adventure or responsibility.
- They are likely to see the world as it is portrayed on the news, as a dangerous place for children to grow.

The Under-supervising Parent

- They say "I don't care" more than they say "No!"
- They are unavailable to coach their child through risky behaviours, unconcerned or too busy to consider the consequences.
- They never warn their child of the bad things that could happen.
- They ignore their past experience with risk and are reluctant to share with their children the lessons they learned.
- They put their needs for calm and routine, or money and adventure, above their child's need for the same.
- They are likely to ignore the real dangers their communities offer their children, blindly doing whatever is good for themselves.

If we're honest, we're all a little overprotective at times, and perhaps a little slack in how we supervise. It is only when we become horribly out of touch with what our risk-taking children are asking that how we parent becomes a problem. Most of us are somewhere between these two extremes, ever-confused and mildly anxious about our children's welfare.

The Concerned Parent

It's not that being more protective, or less willing to supervise your child's every move is right or wrong. Each child's temperament is going to be different. Each child's need to hear the four coveted messages is also going to be different depending on the child's age and mood. And then there's where we live. Each of our communities will present more or less risk to our children. The important thing to do when parenting a child who is a risk-taker is to strive for the right match between:

- What the child says he or she needs
- What you, the parent, thinks the child needs
- The real risks the child faces
- The amount of control the parent wants
- The amount of risk the parent is willing to offer

The concerned parent is one who accepts that his job is to help children experience the right amount of risk. The concerned parent offers her child opportunities to experience risk and responsibility appropriately managed to fit with the child's community and culture. The concerned parent helps his child hear the four messages. The concerned parent is there to coach his child during times of danger.

Do Something Different

Look in the mirror. *Really* look in the mirror! Now imagine your child all grown up. Would you wish your life on them? What parts do you think would be wonderful for them to experience? What parts would you like to spare them?

Now consider . . . you are your child's mirror. She looks to you to find out who she is just as much as as parents we discover who we are through our children. Ask yourself, am I modelling for my child the very best way of living? Am I providing her with the right amount of risk and responsibility to help her make her life as good as mine or better?

Children will either imitate their parents (more than parents ever imagine) or react to everything that a parent hates about herself, living their lives as their family's polar opposite. Either way, the child models her life on what she learns at home.

If looking in the mirror you see a man or woman full of fear and anxiety, then your child will have that to emulate. If looking in the mirror you see caring and tolerance, and a willingness to let others be their very best selves, then that is who your child will become.

Do something good for yourself. Take a vacation from your worry for just one day. Let your child see a different you. Ask yourself, "If I wasn't so anxious today about my children and the risks they were taking, what would I do with my time and energy?"

For a day, do something you imagined you would do if you didn't have to worry so much. Get out of the house (hire a babysitter if you must, but get out!). Have some fun. Spend time and energy focusing on the needs of your spouse. Laugh. Rent the movie you've wanted to see and tell the kids to go and read while you watch it.

Be good to yourself.

Remember, your children are watching. They are watching you to learn how to love themselves and others. They are watching you to understand what it means to be a good parent. They are watching you to understand how to take risks and act responsibly in ways that endanger no one.

TRIALS AND ERRORS

Of course, parenting means letting go just as often as holding our children's hands. Through trial and error our children should figure out for themselves what is and is not dangerous. Otherwise they are likely to grow up experiencing courtroom trials and the errors in judgment that get them there.

It may be one of the most challenging things we do as parents, but we must let our children encounter manageable amounts of risk. For it is those who are least exposed who are most in danger. What problem peers and dangerous adults offer is likely to be far more threatening than what children may have been asking for from their caregivers in the first place.

THE JOY OF RISK

Stress experts have been telling us the positive things about risk-taking behaviour for decades. Risk-taking, at least in manageable amounts, is actually good for us. In the foreword to Peter G. Hanson's[22] *The Joy of Stress*, his friend Sir Edmund Hillary, leader of the first team to reach the summit of Mount Everest, writes that there has always been an element of danger in what he has done: "If there hadn't been, I doubt if I would have gone to the trouble. Danger is stimulating and makes the effort worthwhile."[23] It's the same for children who despite our best efforts to make them behave come up with creative, frequently destructive ways of finding something powerful to say about themselves and living vibrantly.

Children are happiest, and most likely to avoid really dangerous behaviours like drug abuse, early sexual activity, truancy, violence, and running away when adults make their worlds a place of challenge and adventure.

RISK-TAKING IS A GAME

Sadly, many of even the most fortunate of our children, those from stable homes and safe communities, surprise us with their choice of violence, truancy, drug abuse, and "I don't care" attitudes. Risk-taking is a game most youth love to play. Cynthia Lightfoot's[24] heady look at the culture of risk-taking among middle-class adolescents has shown us that for many youth risk-taking is nothing but play, a game that brings with it opportunities to impress peers and adults alike. In fact, Lightfoot tells us, kids prefer taking risks when the odds of succeeding are stacked slightly against them. Under those circumstances, success is that much sweeter, that much more likely to get them noticed by those who are out there watching and applauding our children's "problem" behaviours.

Besides, even for the lucky ones, those with interests and passions, talents and supports, conventional displays of acceptable risk-taking behaviour may bring only temporary status. Many of these children experience their success as precarious. The motto "You're only as good as your last game" frightens them. Many young athletes I meet tell me they are anxious about using *only* their athletic abilities to evoke from others the four messages of "You Belong," "You're Trustworthy," "You're Responsible," and "You're Capable." Sure, their teams may accept them, and for some those moments of glory and belonging are powerful illustrations of all that they are capable of being. But even these shining moments may not be enough.

What then *is* enough? Too often, overzealous parents of really successful children are so proud, and so invested, both emotionally and financially, in their children's success, it is difficult for them to back off, let their child quit, or at least take some time away from an activity to try something new.

When we have been hardened by experience, tested to our limits and survived, we have something special to say about ourselves. It is this self-definition as powerful and competent that will see us through the next time our world unravels.

If risk-taking is a game our children play, then we had better make sure we are offering acceptable risks that are just as much fun as street-driven ones. These can range from the conventional to the downright crazy. It's not really for anyone but a child and the child's family to figure out what's right. Over the years I've become a big fan, for instance, of skateboard parks for children who love spills and thrills. And rock concerts for teenaged boys and girls who want to taste independence and identify themselves with a counterculture. Motorbikes and dirt tracks may be dangerous but are far less so than stolen cars and police chases. Having a boyfriend or girlfriend who parents have met and practising safe sex is better than having a boyfriend or girlfriend parents don't know about and practising unsafe sex. Travelling by oneself to visit or live with a relative in another city is better than hanging out with the homeless when home doesn't feel so comfortable any more. Getting high bungee jumping would be my choice over getting high on drugs. Working as a computer tech on weekends may be better than striving for A's, when all a child really wants is financial freedom, not a university scholarship. Even drinking with one's parents can sometimes be a rite of passage that removes a child's need to sneak a drink with friends.

At some point our children have to taste danger. The kids who drift into lives of conformity and rigid order are setting themselves up for a midlife crisis. Far better, I think, that our children learn to fail a little when they're young than experience far bigger failures for which they're not prepared as adults.

• 5 •

RECKLESS CHILDREN

Some parents expect too much from their children, others too little. Parents who expect too much are constantly telling their kids what to think, what to believe, and how to behave. The neglected kids have no one looking over their shoulder, making sure they succeed. Both patterns of parenting cause children to grow up at risk of becoming reckless with their minds, bodies, and spirits. There is a third way, that of the concerned parent. If we want to help our youth cope with life's challenges, we need to find a respectful, nurturing place in our children's lives.

WHEN CHILDREN ARE NEGLECTED

Meeting Laura-lee, it's easy to see why those who knew the girl when she was younger used to think she was intelligent, competent, even mature. She can still appear to be much older than her fifteen years, which may explain why she has a boyfriend who is eighteen. But people now are more likely to worry aloud about Laura-lee than to heap praise on her.

Laura-lee, her younger brother and two sisters, and her parents, Janice and Roger, live in a small but quaint winterized cottage on a lake just outside a small town. Her parents are well-educated artists whose lifestyle was once trendy. Now they just look out of place in a community that has seen land prices skyrocket. Laura-lee finds her parents and their home an embarrassment. "Why can't my folks just be normal?" she told me during one of our scheduled meetings after she'd been placed in foster care. My job was to help find a way to get Laura-lee to return home. She and I both weren't sure it would work for long if she did.

Laura-lee is a paradox. She was an "A" student until two years before I met her. That's when she and her mother were in a bad car accident. Janice can't stop blaming herself for having been drunk and almost killing them both. Following the accident, Janice was unable to cope with four children and a husband who lay about all day unwilling and unable to help around the house. She'd left for a time, determined to dry out and get her life back together. Meanwhile, responsibility for the house, the younger children, even Roger, was all heaped on Laura-lee's shoulders.

Janice and Roger had both been raised in the suburbs of Boston. They still held the values of the middle class. On some level, they and their children knew that a lifestyle that had worked for the couple when they had no children was failing to meet their children's needs the older they got. Eventually, Social Services had to step in and provide Laura-lee and Roger with what help they could while Janice was in detox. It had been a rough few months for everyone.

It was while she was left with her dad that Laura-lee's behaviour changed. She began hanging out with kids known for their delinquent behaviour, skipping school, disobeying curfews. More than once the police were at Laura-lee's door, either asking where she was, or bringing her home with a warning to behave. Add to this Laura-lee's sexual activity and suspected drug use, and one can quickly see why people had come to see a child in immediate danger and very much at risk of having bigger problems later on.

Janice finally returned home, but by that point she could no more control Laura-lee than Roger, who, to be honest, had never really tried. Almost a year after her return, Janice finally exploded. She'd found Laura-lee on the main street of the small town near their home one afternoon when she should have been in school. Janice had become frustrated when she was unable to get Laura-lee to obey her and come home. Months of tension had worn her down. She gave her daughter a beating right there in public. Laura-lee ran away bruised and bleeding, onlookers called the police, and Janice was jailed for the night. She was put on probation, and Laura-lee placed in foster care with her aunt.

It's tricky knowing how much control to hand over to a teenager like Laura-lee. Even more tricky when a teen like Laura-lee appears to have the capacity to look after herself, but is doing everything she can to make it look like she's messing up royally. When I finally met Laura-lee, she had been allowed weekend visits with her mom and dad, and the situation had improved slightly. Laura-lee and Janice came to counselling with very different expectations. Not surprisingly, it took us some time to work things out.

Laura-lee wanted to be back home with her brothers and sisters, but her mother still harboured a deep resentment about what had happened. Janice blamed the girl for, as she put it, "making me hit her."

While Laura-lee sounds like the kind of out-of-control teen that some think plague our communities, she was actually doing a pretty good job of looking after herself given what she had to work with. When she was younger, being known as a neglected child who was the victim of her parents' incapacity had worked to her advantage. She just had to show up, perform like the rest of the kids, and look after herself, and her teachers, counsellors, and parents were easy to convince she was something special. But with time, and too many problems, she'd simply become fed up with playing the role of the neglected child who makes good. She'd tired of all the pressure to keep up appearances. She had simply resolved to find something better for herself, something that did away with the stigma of being the daughter of an alcoholic mother and an unemployable father.

While some children may have stayed in school and found a way to escape their destiny, Laura-lee just got fed up feeling like all she did was meet others' expectations of her. She didn't want to be the good kid because the good kid was looking ahead at a pretty mediocre life. As she entered adolescence, she wanted more fun and more adventure. She also wanted to be responsible for others, but not in the way that burdened her with chores at home. She wanted to be depended on emotionally, to use all that she had learned growing up so fast. That's where her friends have proven to be so helpful. Laura-lee has a nice, light-hearted way about her, and her friends appreciate the role she plays when she's among them.

"They trust me, that's all," she said to me one day at my office. "They know they can tell me anything and I won't tell anyone." They can also trust her to look after them. She's the non-designated designated driver who makes sure her closest friends don't make stupid decisions, even driving them home unlicensed and underage in cars the kids "borrow" from their parents. And while she stays away from drugs, she hangs close with kids that abuse. She knows others think she's a druggie, guilty by association. The accident she was in, the abuse by her mother, time on the street, it's all made her choose a uniquely different lifestyle that fits for her.

Of course, most people would think, "She's lying" or I'm being conned, that Laura-lee *is* an out-of-control teen who needs some discipline. Maybe, maybe not. You see, what's important to me is to find out how the child *wants others to see her*. Once I know that, I am much better positioned to help the child find safer ways to have the same adventure and responsibility she finds through behaviours that put her in danger and at risk.

Besides, why shouldn't I believe Laura-lee? There's a lot of power to be had being in with a group that abuses while you are the one who stays straight. There's a sensibility in Laura-lee that her parents can't see, and have never really asked their daughter to explain. Laura-lee knows her grades have slipped. "Too distracted, that's all," was how she put it. But she's doing what she has to to stay out of harm's way, avoiding drugs or an early pregnancy. Even if we think otherwise, Laura-lee is convinced she's doing okay.

I meet youth like Laura-lee much more frequently now that I am looking for these stories of hope and resilience. Youth like Laura-lee are often indistinguishable from more troubled peers until we sort the wheat from the chaff. It is up to us adults to ask children to tell us about their worlds, rather than assuming all is as dangerous as it seems. We need to pause and take the time to understand how our children maintain control both of their lives and of the labels others slap on them. And slap them with labels we do!

WHAT ARE THE ODDS?

It was a welcome relief to many professionals, and to many more families, when it became respectable to acknowledge children's success stories rather than doing what we've always done best, giving children names like "at-risk," "latchkey," "neglected," and "abused." Those names, accurate as they may be, come with some heavy baggage. They all imply the child will be a failure.

Fortunately, a growing number of experts the world over are beginning to look at the remarkably large number of children who not only survive great adversity, but thrive as a consequence. These children have come to be known by a different label, one that carries hope – "resilient."

Ann Masten, a leading resilience researcher and psychologist, is today as enthralled with these children as her mentor, Norman Garmezy, was two decades earlier. Masten says that resilience isn't something exceptional, but in fact occurs in the "ordinary magic"[25] of lives lived well under stress. Small decisions, mild acts of courage, unnoticed efforts to survive are often the pathways followed by children who succeed despite the odds against them.

Masten and others like her have discovered that a number of these children, anywhere from ten to upwards of 60 per cent, depending on how resilience is defined and outcomes measured, show a surprising capacity to cope well despite all the problems in their lives. If you are the parent of a child like Laura-lee, a child "at risk," then you may be comforted to know the odds of her turning out just fine are in the child's favour. In fact, as Terri Moffitt has shown through a twenty-year study in New Zealand, 95 per cent of delinquent adolescents stop their problem behaviours by age eighteen.[26]

The trouble is that as children's parents, caregivers, educators, mentors, and even, when things go terribly wrong, their jailors, we haven't fully appreciated the way children use their risk-taking behaviours to carve out for themselves a niche as survivors who thrive. We might also be surprised to learn, if we listen closely, that children experience the alternatives we offer them to risk-taking behaviours as boring, isolating solutions that bring nothing but control by others, conformity, mediocrity, and criticism for not measuring up to those who are more perfect.

TEACHING CHILDREN CONTROL OVER THEIR MINDS, BODIES, AND SPIRITS

For most of the last one hundred years, psychologists have believed that those cute cherub-looking babies we hold in our arms become violent out-of-control teens because of what happens to them as they grow up or because of some internal flaw in their personalities. We have blamed parents, and the children themselves, government policies, and peers. New research, however, by Richard Tremblay and his colleagues at the Université de Montreal[27] has shown that children are actually their most violent and reckless selves when they are babies. Children don't grow up becoming bad. Growing up provides children with the opportunities they need to curb their aggressive tendencies and socialize themselves into well-behaved adults. Imagine if you will a two-year-old in a sixteen-year-old's body. Tremblay ruefully describes this large baby as nothing less than a monster, ready to destroy his parents, hit, bite, tear, and break anything in his path when his needs are thwarted. Fortunately for us, babies are seldom that lethal because we can hold and restrain them.

Our children's reckless behaviours are similar. The secure, well-attached child will naturally explore his world with abandonment, likely putting himself constantly in harm's way. Recklessness is not something we grow into, it is inside us from the start. Our role as caregivers, Tremblay reminds us, is to teach children appropriate ways to get what they want. The reckless baby grows up to be the responsible and cautious teen because of what his parents and caregivers offer him.

All Laura-lee really wanted was to have some say over her body, her mind, and her spirit. The older she got, the more elusive these simple goals appeared to become. As she went looking for fun, freedom, and the right to control her own body, there was no one there to help her in those pursuits. Laura-lee didn't become reckless. She was happily reckless all along. Only, for a time, she tamed her reckless behaviour because conformity and good grades had brought her the messages she wanted to hear. She could convince herself she belonged, was responsible, trustworthy, and capable. What's more, she survived well because she also managed to make herself a competent, caring contributor to her community.

Children are their most reckless selves at birth. Our role as caregivers is to provide appropriate, less destructive ways for children to express their recklessness.

As long as she played along and fit in as the good little girl from the problem family, everyone was happy. But once she started saying, "I want to think for myself," all hell broke loose. No surprise, really. Laura-lee had received very little coaching along the way on how to keep safe. If she had tamed her reckless impulses for a time, it was because she could see the benefits. Once those benefits disappeared, there was really no point being so self-contained.

PARENTS NEED TO BE COACHES

If Laura-lee teaches us the danger of too little supervision, then I don't have to look much further than my street to witness how the mania of parents to keep their children safe is endangering them as much as Laura-lee's parents endangered her with their lack of super-vision. Like under-supervision, overprotection is harming our children more than we are ready to admit.

Fred, a friend of mine, tells me how incredible he finds it that his teenaged daughter's friends know nothing about keeping safe in the city. "Honestly, what are their parents thinking," he said one day over a beer while we were waiting for friends to join us at a local pub. "It drives me crazy watching them skateboard in the middle of the road. Or walk out from between parked cars. And I'm not talking about little kids either. Yesterday, I almost clipped these two girls by the high school who couldn't be bothered to use the crosswalk.

Lucky for them I wasn't going just a bit faster. So few of them have any street sense whatsoever. They're complete and utter hazards, to themselves, and to everyone else as well." He waved his arms frantically in front of his face, as if he could somehow wipe the memory away with a simple gesture.

He may have been exaggerating. He's a bit like that. But his point is well taken. He'd been concerned enough for his children's safety that he'd taught them early what they needed to know about city streets. I'd faced the same challenge with my own children. If they were going to grow up in the city, I had reasoned like Fred, they had better know how to survive in a city.

HOW A CONCERNED PARENT CAN HELP

Concerned parents strive to balance the amount of protection they offer with their child's need for freedom to explore his world on his own terms. Concerned parents are effective at negotiating the right amount of protection and the right amount of risk for their children. They're effective because they:

1. Listen to what their children say they need and find ways to meet those needs
2. Honour what they know as parents and do what they think is right for their children
3. Are willing to ask themselves honestly if the risks they perceive are really risks at all
4. Are willing to give up some control to their children for decisions the children can handle themselves
5. Are happy to provide both the opportunities to experience some risk and the coaching to help their children succeed

Do Something Different

Celebrate your successes. Every parent has lots of reasons to be proud of their accomplishments raising their children. The late nights, the hand-holding, the birthday parties with the chocolate cake and extra icing just the way your child wanted it. The band-aids, both the plastic kind and the emotional ones as well. The hugs. In times of crisis and conflict, we can forget just how important we've been to our children.

Now that they're teenagers, our work is far from done. Ask yourself, "When did I last permit my child to take some risk? Assume some responsibility?" Every family has their own special way of helping children grow into competent adults. In my clinical work, I always find it simpler to *encourage families to do more of what already works* rather than jumpstart entirely new behaviour. If you encouraged your child to be brave and go to school at five, and despite her trepidation and your own, the child went, then that same child is likely to trust you when you offer to help her get off your couch and get a job or dump her abusive boyfriend.

A simple rule to follow is: Do more of what's already worked; do less of what hasn't.

Okay, so you know what you did right when your children were small. Most parents, however, find it difficult to turn lessons learned with children at age five into strategies for managing their teenagers. To make it easier, consider the following:

- Listen to your child when she tells you what she needs. The thirteen-year-old who says, "I want a boyfriend" or "You never let me go to any parties" is telling you she's ready to be an adult and assume adult-sized risks. It makes sense that if you used to do birthday parties in ways that pleased your child, you'd do well to continue the tradition and make her next party co-ed. At the very least, you'll be able to discuss with your daughter beforehand what is acceptable and unacceptable behaviour in your home. Find a compromise that suits you both. One family I know agreed that during their daughter's first co-ed party, the parents would stay in the kitchen as long as the lights stayed on in the living room and there was no going into any of the bedrooms or the basement. Mom played short-order cook. Dad put coats away. The girl organized everything else just the way she wanted it.

- Build scaffolding around whatever personality your child is trying to create. If he's into being a gangsta rapper, then why not provide access to rap lessons and breakdancing workshops, both available through many local youth clubs. After all, thinking back, when your child was seven and said he wanted to play guitar, did you buy him a guitar or say "No!" and force him to study chess? Any activity your child wants to try, no matter how much you might disagree with it, usually has a more acceptable form of expression.
- Let him decorate his room in whatever way he wants. Many parents are just fine with their children choosing the drawings they pin to their bulletin boards when preschoolers. Then the children become teens, but parents still insist on neat and tidy, or reds and blues, while their child is begging to decorate all their walls with murals of black swirling dragons and mascara-laden witches. Far from disappointing, this should be seen for what it is, a sign of successful parenting, the preschooler now ready to take on more responsibility and express himself through his surroundings. Remember, you don't really have to look at those walls, and paint can always be covered with two coats of primer when the teenager becomes a young man.

ASK BEFORE TELLING

If we are going to influence our children's choice of risk-taking behaviour, we are first going to have to tidy up how we communicate with them. After all, let's be honest, how many of us really listened to our parents when they gave us good advice? And yet, here we are surprised when our children resist our sage direction.

Meeting with families in distress has brought with it some lessons from the trenches of parenting. As I've watched families cope with risk-taking children, time and again, I've learned that the adults who are most helpful ask themselves a few simple questions before jumping to the conclusion their child needs them to tell her what to do.

When thinking about children's risk-taking behaviours, stop and ask yourself:

1. Whose problem is the child's behaviour?
2. Is the child being challenged with the right amount of risk?
3. Who's going to notice the child's success?

These three questions are crucial to understanding why our children continue taking risks even after we warn them not to. Whether their risk-taking behaviour is socially desirable or undesirable, children are at a great advantage growing up if they take risks and survive.

Still, it's difficult for parents who strive to balance concern with direction to watch as children throw themselves headlong into risky situations. Monkey bars become downtown bars. Our children's choice of friends can be controlled at four but are well beyond our control at fourteen. Suddenly we are nothing more than coaches on the sidelines. Oh, how we long to be back in the game, calling the plays!

Catrina, the eldest daughter of friends of mine, worried her family sick when she packed up her knapsack and, at the youthful age of seventeen, used her own savings to pay her way to Europe. For years, she'd been working at Tim Hortons evenings and weekends, learning about being independent while she served her regulars coffee and their favourite donuts. Needless to say, her parents were beside themselves, anxious about how she would ever survive on her own in a foreign country.

But Catrina had spunk. She also had her own passport, money, and the defiance to challenge anyone who told her what she could and couldn't do. The defiant child is also the child most likely to tell her peers what they can do with their rules. When dealing with a child like Catrina as she makes her way into adulthood, we might do well to consider the three questions listed above each in its own turn.

The first question
"Whose problem is the child's behaviour?" For Catrina, there was no problem. She felt ready to take on this challenge. It was her parents who were full of fear. But what were they afraid of, exactly?

Maybe Catrina was too young to travel by herself, but this was the rite of passage she had chosen. Eventually, Catrina's parents realized the problem was theirs, not their daughter's. It was their fear that was imposing itself and threatening to ruin a good relationship. To Catrina's mind, she was ready to launch herself out into the world. Hadn't she shown as much by holding a job, saving her money, acting in all ways more adult-like than many adults?

It's not unusual for parents to make their children's problems their own. At a party during the Christmas holidays the woman sitting beside me lamented, "My twelve-year-old is causing me so much work. She changes her clothes five times a day. I mean it, five times a day! Well, I put an end to that. She can change her clothes twice. That's all. *I'm not going to be picking up her things five times in one day."*

I sat there my mouth agape. I shouldn't have said anything, I know, but sometimes my mouth gets in gear before my brain is engaged.

"Maybe you could teach her to do her own laundry? Then she could change her clothes as often as she liked," I suggested, trying to sound nonchalant, but I'm pretty sure the woman could hear the smugness in my voice. It was a wasted effort anyway.

"Oh no, she'd never agree to that. She'd just pile the clothes on the floor until she had none, then what would *I* do? She'd be going to school and be in ugly sweats. She'd do it too, just to prove her point."

I still couldn't see the problem. But then I'm all for making sure my children's problems don't become mine. I'm all for giving them the skills and the coaching to help them *solve their problems themselves.* It's easier, I find, to share responsibility with them. I understand my role is to get them ready to be adults by the ripe young age of eighteen. That includes both making decisions about what they wear and doing their own laundry.

The second question
Thinking back to Catrina, the second question we need to ask ourselves as parents is *"Is she being challenged with the right amount of risk?"*

A risk that is manageable is also one which is well-timed. Any intervention with a child has to be matched to the child's physical and emotional development. In fact, risk-taking that fits with what a child can be reasonably expected to succeed at is always the best kind of risk-taking. But who decides? Who knows when a child is ready? And who knows the full scope of the danger the child is placing herself into?

There's no easy way to find the right answers to these questions. There is simply no substitute for listening to each other and reaching a compromise. It's easier than you think. Most children hold a cherished secret they don't like shared with us adults. *Children are quite happy to heed the advice of well-meaning parents when those same parents are willing to own up to their part turning risk-taking behaviour into problems.*

Once Catrina's family understood they had much more fear about their daughter's safety than she did, they were willing to work with their daughter on a plan to keep her safe, but still let her have her adventure. Catrina picked up on her parents' different way of seeing her and was more than happy (and maybe even relieved) to do things that would reassure her family while at the same time making her travel safer.

As a compromise, Catrina agreed to check in with a friend of the family's who lived in England, and the niece of a neighbour who was working in Germany. And she'd call, as often as possible.

Fortunately, Catrina survived quite well. In fact, she came home sooner than expected. Seems lonely train rides and endless lunches of baguettes and cheese are not nearly as attractive as they might seem from a distance.

The third question

Finally, we need to ask, *"Who's going to notice the child's success?"* Lots of people had noticed how responsible Catrina was working at the Tim Hortons. But to Catrina's mind, that recognition had long ago worn thin. She wanted to impress herself, her parents, and her friends by showing them what she could really do. She wanted to make sure they would see her not only as an adult, but also as an adventurer!

And they did notice. She returned with stories to tell about romantic moments on trains, about seedy hostels in Paris's Montmartre district, about Italian touts that almost stole all her money. She talked about meeting other young women from Australia and Japan. Best of all, she wove together a story about herself as a survivor. Her trip had been a calculated, slightly edgy risk that had left her feeling ready for bigger challenges, even if it had raised her parents' blood pressure and driven them a little mad with anxiety.

As I like to tell children whom I meet through my practice, "Raising parents is very difficult!"

It might help us to relax a bit if we think back to our own child-hoods. Much of what we think of as risk-taking behaviour today was just normal growth and development for children generations ago in our own country, and still is today in many others. To many people around the world, Catrina's desire to leave home on her own adven-ture would not seem so odd. In the early 1900s, my wife's grand-mother became a missionary's wife at seventeen and shortly after was steaming towards China. We joke that if she had been living a hundred years later, she would simply have done what Catrina did. She may never have taken up a religious vocation, or more likely, she would have waited a little longer.

But none of that was done then. The door to adventure for my wife's grandmother fit her particular time and place. There is no getting around it. What is a risk to one person at one point in time will not be a risk to someone else living in a different community, at a different time, and with different values.

How do we so easily forget as adults what it was like for us when we were children? It is as if we have a collective amnesia. We are unable, or perhaps unwilling, to remember all that we were capable of doing at an early age.

WHEN THEIR PROBLEM BECOMES OUR PROBLEM

Sometimes, unfortunately, children's problems become their parents' problems. Let's face it, if Catrina had come to harm in Europe it would have been her parents flying to the rescue. That's why it is so important to ask ourselves if the risks our children face are *manage-able* and *well-timed*. Of course, as outsiders to our children's worlds, we will never be able to answer that question alone. We need to

"AFFLUENZA"

The most fortunate of lower-class families live in "high context" communities, communities with a strong social network of supports. In fact, it is often in middle- and upper-class communities where we find the dark and hidden realities of youth who are ignored, desperate for something good to say about themselves. The problem for many families is not a lack of money, but the fact that wealth alone is not making children any healthier. In fact, ironically, excessive wealth can be a threat to children's happiness when parents fail to provide meaning as well as financial security.

Sometimes called "affluenza," this catchy phrase coined by John de Graaf,[28] describes the disease of affluence affecting children who have grown up with expectations that the wealth they experience will bring happiness. What they seldom see, and their parents avoid making them experience, is the work it takes to succeed. In other words, children who are provided with too many things are denied the identity that comes from the satisfaction of creating one's own wealth, of taking chances, and assuming responsibility both for oneself and others. Without the work half of the life–satisfaction equation, children have only an identity as someone who enjoys conspicuous consumption. They go from one purchase to the next, chameleons of fashion and style. These children are unable to assert themselves. They struggle to say, "This is who I am" because they have little chance to opt out of the designer lifestyle that is forced upon them.

The result is a whole bunch of unhappy, unfulfilled children who will do the darnedest things to find adventure and responsibility. Suniya Luthar, a child psychologist, has documented the cost of affluence, reporting the lowest levels of happiness among the most affluent of children.[29] How can that be? Less family time, and a lack of closeness with high-achieving parents are Luthar's best guesses as to the causes. I think she may, however, have overlooked the lack of meaning and purpose a Paris Hilton lifestyle brings with it.

Maybe that's why as a group this population is also *more likely* to use drugs than the poor kids who are the dealers. In fact, one of the best predictors that a child will use drugs is a weekly allowance of twenty-five dollars or more. When you have no other way to prove yourself, drugs can look like a wonderful solution. Marijuana, inhalants, and tranquilizers are all common drugs among the wealthy. The same for smoking and drinking. Add the club drugs MDMA, Ketamine, and Rohypnol, as well as whatever drugs are left over in the kids' own bathroom cabinets from treatments for ADHD and the like, and we can quickly see that the most privileged youth are also those with the most opportunity to abuse their bodies. Luthar's study also shows that affluent kids report higher levels of anxiety and depression. Making matters even worse is the absence of other ways to strut their stuff. Peers, especially male peers of affluent children, love to heap praise on the kids who drink and do drugs to excess.

Of course, children from affluent homes have the option of making their lives more meaningful. They can take advantage of opportunities to be something more than their next pair of trendy low-rider jeans. But it's not easy. If they opt out they pay the price of being a social outcast. It is a price few who get trapped in the "I am what I buy" culture of wealthy suburbs are willing to pay. Children who go from one purchase to the next wind up feeling empty even if they are well pampered. They need parents to offer them something more genuine. They need opportunities to experience risk and responsibility.

The solution is not to take it all away, removing children's bedroom televisions, denying them their own cars, refusing them school trips to the French Alps. These ideas are likely to cross the minds of concerned wealthy parents. There must be *substitutes*, however, offering children choices that are every bit as stimulating as the immediate pleasures of consumerism. This is where most affluent parents get stuck. It baffles them why their children should have to take risks, suffer as much as they did to reach the heights of success they achieved. These parents can't imagine substituting rites of passage that put their children in any appreciable danger. It's what they've worked so hard to eradicate.

Ironic, isn't it? Kids are hard-wired to need the very thing many parents strive to free them from – the chance to learn, through taking on risk and responsibility, how to be competent, caring contributors to their communities who everyone admires.

consult the kids. Are they ready for the risks they have chosen? Parenting guru Barbara Coloroso would have us ask our children to *convince us* that they are ready to take on any challenge they choose.

Keeping children safe, and helping them navigate opportunities for growth is as much our children's responsibility as it is our responsibility as their parents to make those opportunities happen.

Children need to shout "This is who I am!" not "This is what I can buy!" The first teaches them the skills to be powerful and self-assured; the second teaches them they are only as good as the image they can buy their way into.

NO PAIN, NO LONG-TERM GAIN

How many of us as parents have advised our children how best to spend their money? I often think to myself that it is better to watch a child mismanage fifty dollars than mismanage five hundred dollars when they're a teenager, or worse, five thousand dollars when they're in their twenties. Though as concerned parents we caution our children that their choices may not be the best, we sometimes need to insist they make mistakes, or at least what looks like a mistake to us. We need to say, "Go ahead, you can buy that. It will use up all your savings, but if it is important to you, then do it." I know these words personally. For thirty-eight dollars, my daughter, when she was just seven, bought the latest Harry Potter toy that thirty-eight *hours* later was left to rot in the corner because it had become boring. But the purchase wasn't a complete waste. My child had discovered the falsehood of marketers. The toy didn't really do what the picture on the box promised. I'm hoping the lesson isn't lost when she's a teenager. After all, someday, those same marketers will pitch to her images of cigarettes and other kinds of harmful products.

I also like to think of this as an immunization for my child against the disease of future credit card debt. If she didn't blow her savings at age seven, and learn to regret it, then that lesson is still waiting to be learned at seventeen and twenty-seven when the stakes are much higher. Allowing children to make wasteful and bad decisions that bring very little long-term pain is the sign of a caring parent who understands that his role is not just to protect, but to help his child learn about life.

Too often we think that the poor urban kids are the ones most at risk. But many of those kids come from more functional families than those higher up the economic ladder. None of this is meant to gloss over the hardships of poverty and the challenges it poses to children. However, to assume that being poor means that kids' families don't work well is to overlook the obvious: children from middle- and upper-class families can be neglected or given the message their lives are meaningless as much as any child growing up in poverty.

> *The right amount of risk brings with it the right amount of recognition. Our problem as adults is to ensure our children balance risk-taking with acceptance-seeking.*

WHAT OUR KIDS REALLY NEED

We need to provide our children (rich or poor) with opportunities to grow through exposure to manageable amounts of risk and responsibility. For example, offering to pay a child's way to work at a summer camp for children with disabilities in the French Alps would be a far more generous offer by a parent than the week-long funfest most are willing to finance. Insisting a child use his or her car to deliver pizza or newspapers in order to pay their own insurance is one way to teach responsibility and to make a child value what he or she owns.

For parents who have the resources to provide for their children, it is important that they provide wisely. Here are a few suggestions based on my work with families who have had to teach their children how to be their best selves in spite of their wealth and privilege:

1. Don't buy it unless they need it. Let children buy what they need themselves by providing them with an allowance or, when older, helping them find work.

2. Buy what they don't need (like a special designer piece of clothing, an expensive piece of sports equipment, or electronics item)

only when you are confident the child isn't using the purchase to say something about herself. Remember, when our possessions become crutches for self-definition, we quickly find ourselves forgetting who we really are.

3. Provide children opportunities to make a contribution. Communities have lots of space for young people who want to give something of themselves to others.

4. Provide opportunities for children to experience lots of different types of people. Remember, they need to practise fitting in if they are going to acquire the skills they need to convince others they are worth knowing on their own terms.

When we define ourselves by our possessions, we quickly need new ones as new becomes old. A self-definition that is as fleeting as the next new trend in electronics or clothing is not going to be an identity that lasts for long.

5. Give of your time more than your pocketbook. When love is in short supply, children will always choose a parent's attention over something bought at the store.

It all comes back to the problem of finding something powerful to say about ourselves. The things we own will come and go, but the feeling of accomplishment that comes with earning something endures. Earning something means assuming responsibility. And it is only through experiences of risk and responsibility that children find ways to hear that they belong, are trustworthy, respected, and competent. Ironically, we need to *reinvent risk* in the lives of our most privileged children in order to provide them with the building blocks for success.

Do Something Different

Think back to your own childhood. How did you learn the value of money? What, if anything, did your parents do to help you understand the need to budget and save, or the value of a hard day's work? Some of us never had those opportunities. Many of us, however, did. I began working the summer I turned twelve, helping take inventory in a factory warehouse my father managed. I know many others like me who have similar stories.

I'll admit I don't expect the same of my own children. But I do expect them to assume some responsibility for their own finances, and have helped them look for opportunities to work a few hours for neighbours and friends.

Consider your own children. How are they learning the same lessons you had to learn? What experiences have you provided them to develop the skills they will need to become financially independent?

Here are a few suggestions from parents with whom I've worked who have helped their children avoid reckless financial decisions:

- Provide children with an allowance that is *not* in payment for household chores. Teaching a child to be a competent, caring contributor to her family means she must understand that no one in her family gets paid to walk the dog, empty the dishwasher, or vacuum the living room. Neither parents nor child. An allowance is about learning how to manage money. It's not a salary. And when a child wants a pair of trendy jeans, or to take in a concert with her friends, she will learn from the experience how to manage her money. Most importantly, she needs to know that when it's gone, it's gone! At least until the next week or month.
- Insist your child work for someone other than you when they are teenagers. Elderly neighbours need walkways cleared of snow, or leaves raked. There's always fence painting and even reading to someone whose eyesight is failing. There's dog walking, and delivering flyers. If none of these opportunities are available, and they may not be in every community, there is always fundraising for a local charity. It doesn't put money in your own child's pocket, but it teaches them responsibility and forces them to develop the social skills they will need to approach a stranger and sell themselves. What better way to build a resume and develop the chutzpah they'll need to impress future employers!
- Open a bank account in the child's name. Most banks have no-fee

youth accounts that are a good way to help children understand what it means to use a bank. Some parents insist a portion of their child's allowance and other income must (1) be saved, and (2) be donated to a charity of her choice. Both are good strategies to teach your child proper money-management skills.

ALL GROWN UP BUT WITH NO COMMON SENSE

A student at my university was caught plagiarizing her assignments four times. When the young woman was to be permanently suspended, her father, a well-known lawyer, came to his daughter's defence. Sure enough, there in the minutiae of legalese there was a clause that prevented the university from expelling the student. Daddy had saved his little girl once again from the consequences of her actions.

But where will the father be when this same young woman gets a job and is still unaware of the consequences to her behaviour? What happens when she commits a more serious breach of trust, perhaps endangering a customer, perhaps embezzling money, perhaps just not showing up on time, or lying about the hours she's worked? Someone, sometime, is going to have to suffer when this young woman meets a challenge she cannot get around without cheating.

What would compel a young person from such a privileged background to do something so foolish as to risk being expelled from university? In my work with young people, good and bad, they tell me they act recklessly when they are searching for a powerful, elusive identity. That student, after all, likely had a lot riding on being everything Daddy expected her to be. Failure was not an option. Reckless disregard for rules seemed to be her best and only solution to get through university, a solution that set her up for tragic consequences. After the disciplinary hearing she returned to her studies but it was obvious her professors didn't trust her. She eventually graduated, but without an academic reference she is unlikely to get into graduate school, something she was clearly expected to do.

Do Something Different

What would you do if it was your daughter who was caught plagiarizing? Of course, many of us would want to defend our child and would use any means at our disposal to protect her. It can be horribly painful for a parent to watch their child fail.

It is much easier to know what to do in such circumstances when we ask ourselves the right questions:

- What kind of adult do I want my child to become?
- How do I want them to behave when they are twenty-five (rather than five or fifteen)?
- What does my child need to learn right now to take the first step towards becoming that person?
- What can I do to support them while they fix their mistakes?
- What can I do to prevent them from getting into even more serious trouble?

The answers to these kinds of questions are likely to encourage a concerned response to a child that allows her to suffer the natural consequences of her risk-taking behaviours while she's still young enough to fix her mistakes.

Showing your concern, however, is only half the solution. You will also have to understand why your child is recklessly endangering herself and possibly others. If she is searching for something powerful to say about herself, and the options are few, then offering a substitute will ensure she doesn't have to keep making the same mistake over and over again. For example, in the case of a child who lies and cheats:

- Offer the child an alternative that doesn't involve lying and cheating. If a twelve-year-old from a small town is sneaking into the big city an hour away on his own or with friends, worrying his parents senseless, maybe it's time to take him downtown for an afternoon and let him and three friends wander the stores with twenty dollars in their pockets, watches on their wrists, and a time to meet at a local McDonald's for a meal. A legitimate adventure that involves some risk is always preferable to the ill-chosen and impulsive behaviour of a child desperate to be taken seriously.

• Model honesty. Tell your child about times you've acted recklessly or bent the rules: driven over the speed limit; not paid for something either accidentally or intentionally; lied about your age or qualifications. Explain the consequences, if there were any. Even if there weren't consequences, you can still talk about your regrets, or what might have happened if you'd been caught.

The goal, remember, is to teach your child how to reason through these problems, not to suppress all risk-taking behaviour. If we show our kids how to think through risky situations, the better prepared they will be to behave safely and responsibly without having to resort to lies and deception.

WHAT HAPPENS WHEN WE TELL CHILDREN TO FIT IN?

Unfortunately, we don't often offer children very good alternatives to the risk-taking behaviours they choose on their own. Mary Pipher's look at the crisis facing young girls, which she wrote about in her bestselling book *Reviving Ophelia*, could just as easily have been titled "Ophelia Denied." Denied adventure, denied a sexuality, denied the right to assert herself, denied a future, denied a way to be recognized as the powerful young women our daughters want to be. To hear girls talk about their lives (and speak they have in countless studies), they hear nothing except what they are told not to do. Girls tell us they hear precious little about anything they are supposed to do that isn't mainstream, socially desirable, ladylike, and safe.

Little wonder we, a generation before, made the choice to opt out of traditional roles rather than fit in. Unfortunately, we seem to have forgotten to pass those values along to our children, both girls and boys. We say we don't want our children to follow the pack, fit in or

CHURCHGOERS ARE VULNERABLE TOO

Children who go to church, synagogue, mosque, shrineroom, or temple, but who never challenge, or are permitted to challenge, the orthodoxy of their elders, are children who will never know the risk-taker's advantage. The child who asks tough questions is the one who is going to be safer in the long run than the one who blindly follows. These challenges to the institutions of religion should be embraced. I don't want children to follow anyone's truth uncritically. I want them to commit to a truth *they* believe in passionately.

When parents bring me children who they say are refusing to attend weekly religious services with them, or who otherwise are rejecting what parents insist is necessary for their child's emotional or spiritual development, I begin by asking parents what they really want for their children. Do they want compliant children who will follow *anyone's* assertion of the truth or children with a zest for life who are willing to think for themselves and then passionately defend truth once they've figured it out? If they are looking for the latter, I challenge them to:

1. Encourage compliant children to try doing something different for a time (that includes attending a different religious institution than the one the family attends).
2. Encourage children to take more responsibility for themselves and their beliefs (can they defend why they believe what they believe?).
3. Encourage children to question the values of those they respect.
4. Teach children appropriate ways to question elders so that defiance doesn't become rudeness.

The family that does these things is more likely to raise a child who suffers less anxiety and feels comfortable becoming a part of the adult world. For the fortunate family whose children show *healthy rebellion,* their behaviour may be nothing more than a sign that parents have given their children the skills to think critically for themselves.

listen to peers, yet we want them to follow us, fit in with what we expect and do as we say.

The boys don't have it much easier than the girls in this regard. But the messages are different. At about the same time Pipher was winding her way through girls' consciousness, William Pollack was trying to understand boys. They too, we learned, are being short-changed, made to mind the rules when many want the freedom that some good old-fashioned adventure and the right to make their own choices would bring.

Do Something Different

Ask yourself how you found your faith. Could anyone have ever forced you to believe what you believe? How have you opened space for your own child to discover her spirituality?

The more we model for our children appropriate ways to take intellectual and spiritual risks, and experiment with many different beliefs, the more likely they are to follow our lead and honour us with respect for what we most value. Try putting in practice the following expressions of tolerance:

- Attend events like marches for peace and other ecumenical celebrations that bring together people with many different values. Showing tolerance for others is the best way to gain the respect of your child.
- If you can afford it, take the time to travel and experience different cultures. Most children will return to their own religious backgrounds once they have experienced the world in ways that others experience it.
- Reassure your child that he can always come back home. Excommunicating a child for his beliefs only ruins the very special relationships children want with their caregivers.

If we don't teach young children to think for themselves and prevent our adult fears from burdening them, then it will be that much harder to teach them to think for themselves when they're teenagers. The little girl Tess has already been told she is wrong to think for herself. Will it be any surprise when she listens to someone else, like an older boy, a music-video star, or maybe just the other girls at school, who will be quick to tell her when she's a teen, "Be just like us." Sex? Why not. Drugs? Sure. There is no shortage of ways Tess can take risks that will be available to her once she navigates her way beyond her parents' front door. Sadly, girls and boys who slide into these troubling behaviours tell me that these other choices bring with them as much admiration, at least temporarily, as being the kind of children they started out wanting to be: gutsy risk-takers out to impress *their parents!*

We teach our children about tolerance and devotion through our tolerance of them and our devotion to what we hold to be the truth. As their parents, we remain their best teachers.

But to draw children away from behaviours that are destructive to themselves and others, we need to offer something that will bring with it as much *recognition* as they already receive from what they are already doing. No wonder we so seldom succeed in finding an acceptable alternative. It's a tall order coming up with a substitute that can compete with our children's love of dangerous behaviour.

It's not impossible, though.

In fact, it's remarkably easy when we understand what our children are trying to find when they behave recklessly. Knowing that puts us in a better position to offer them an appropriate alternative, one they'll like and embrace as their own.

·6·

RISK? WHAT RISK?

Time moves on, children grow up to be parents, and somewhere
along the way forget what it was like to be a kid. They forget
what it was like to embrace adventure, to seek responsibility beyond
our years.

I was having dinner with some friends one New Year's Eve and as
the clock counted down yet another year, I asked everyone whether
children today are more at risk than when we were kids? There was a
collective sigh, and then a barrage of opinions. Most of us could tell
stories about the risks we were routinely exposed to that we would
never expose our own children to. We were put out in the morning
and told not to come back until lunch. We were allowed to ride
motorcycles unsupervised at age twelve. We walked alone to school.
Most of us were expected to see to it that our homework was done
without much supervision from our parents. In fact, few of us could
remember parents with enough time to ever ask us "Is it done yet?"

And yet, almost to a person, everyone around that table also
believed that children today need to be more protected, that children
today live in a world *more dangerous* than the one we grew up in.
Maybe that's because more than ever before we *perceive* the risks our
children face. We hear about them more. We suffer the maelstrom of
twenty-four-hour news networks that both tell us about the world

and shape our place in it. All of a sudden our quiet communities are potentially dangerous places. As one mother said, "We all worry about the *random maniac*," the crazed child killer who is lurking just beyond our front door.

It may not be popular to say it, but the statistical likelihood of that random maniac being in your community is far less today than at any other time in history. If we are convinced our children are more at risk, we might want to start by asking ourselves, "How do we know this?" When we were younger, did every random act of violence against a child *anywhere in the world* find its way into our dinner conversation? I don't remember it being like that in my house. Nor do most of the adults who grew up around me who now worry about their children walking alone at any age.

Before we can look seriously at substitutes for children's destructive risk-taking behaviours, we need to take a second look at whether our children are really at as much risk as we want to believe they are. After all, there's no point seeking alternatives if you believe the cure is worse than the disease! If you are a parent who believes that there is more danger out there for your child today than there was for you when you were growing up, this chapter may provide some surprises.

SEARCHING FOR FUN BUT FINDING DANGER INSTEAD

Calvin, a boy who lives down the street from me, was given a new fibreglass bow and three steel-tipped arrows for his twelfth birthday. I watched curiously from my front deck one hot summer afternoon as his father coached him on its proper use. Dad had even made a target out of an old Styrofoam cooler, painted a bull's eye on the bottom, and placed it by some front-yard trees. The serious look on Dad's face told me that Calvin was being ordered in no uncertain terms to mind the rules or he'd lose the bow.

Predictably, once Dad had gone back inside, Calvin couldn't resist the temptation to see how far he could shoot an arrow. After the first shot, he realized that the bigger the arc, the farther the arrows went. It wasn't long before Calvin almost took out the window of a neighbour's car and Dad was back outside threatening the boy that the bow would be put away for a long time unless he stuck to the rules and shot the arrows only where he was supposed to shoot.

I took another sip of soda on my front deck and waited.

Left on their own, our children will take risks to prove themselves. Given opportunities to channel their enthusiasm, they will likely follow our lead and agree to safer ways to express themselves.

Calvin, figuring his way through this dilemma, seemed to decide that if he wanted to see how far he could shoot an arrow, he didn't need to shoot into the neighbour's yard. Creatively, he figured out that he could shoot straight up. That way, he wouldn't really be breaking Dad's rules, now would he? I watched him concentrate hard and then, before I could put down my drink and shout over some neighbourly advice, Calvin sent that arrow far enough up into the sky that he lost sight of it. That's when his expression changed. You could see on his face that he had just figured out the problem with what he'd just done. He had no idea where that arrow was going to land.

Now, don't get me wrong, this could have ended badly, and I'm certainly not advocating letting children make such potentially dangerous decisions. But Calvin's problem wasn't his alone to solve. And thankfully, the whole episode didn't end in tragedy. Calvin stood there and waited. You could see his relief (and mine too) when the arrow broke through the top branches of one of the trees in his yard. I laughed at his folly, and was certain he wouldn't soon try such a silly trick again.

But I also found myself afterwards wondering why Dad didn't take the boy out to a field and let him shoot an arrow as far as he could? Wouldn't that have been a better way to help the boy experience the adventure of his new "toy"?

Still, score one for all the children who have had to learn things the hard way. Score another for Calvin himself who figured out that his actions have consequences, for himself and for others.

GROWING UP IN A LESS PERFECT TIME

The challenge for parents is how to create vivid opportunities for personal growth without necessarily endangering life and limb. It was as much a challenge for our parents as it is for us today. Only, it seems when we were young, we had more ways to assert ourselves and deal with the risks that came along. We walked to school, which meant more time to spend with friends and opportunities to learn how to cross busy streets. We were in unsupervised sporting activities most days, not the scheduled club dates children now experience. We were much more likely to work at part-time jobs. We were expected to do more around the house. We even had to make our own Halloween costumes and Christmas presents. Our lives were more under our control than our children feel theirs are today.

Our children need families and communities who are watching, but not oversimplifying, their lives.

I'm not nostalgic for a time when everything was perfect. Quite the contrary. I'm nostalgic for a time when things were *less perfect*, when children still had opportunities to prove themselves. If it appears that our children today are more violent, doing more drugs, becoming sexually active earlier, it's because we are worried about them more than ever before. With our communities as safe as they are, we should be extending to our children *more* opportunities to take risks. Instead we are shrinking their worlds, burdening them with our adult fears.

Our children need the same kind of challenges we had as kids. But they also need the support of caring adults who can help them cope. Our children are begging us for opportunities to prove themselves.

Do Something Different

How many of us adults sit with a coffee clutched between our hands and lament, "If only . . ." If only our parents had offered us that special moment of their time to understand us better. If only our parents had provided us with substitutes for our own dangerous, delinquent, deviant, and disordered behaviour. Who among us didn't at some point learn from the school of hard knocks?

Now consider your role as parent. How will your child grade your performance? When was the last time she asked something of you and you denied her what she wanted *without offering a substitute*?

The next time your child asks you for help taking risks (I want to attend the concert, in another city, just with my friends) or responsibility in excess of what you think she can handle ("My boss wants me to work this weekend until 2 a.m."), don't say "No!" Instead, sit down with your child and brainstorm at least *two* possible options that will make it more likely for you to say "Yes" and still be sure she's safe.

- Want to attend a concert out-of-town? Then what about your daughter and her friends staying with her Aunt Louise (or a family friend). You'll know they're safe even if Aunt Louise is a little wacky and irresponsible. The kids will have their adventure, and it will give you some peace of mind.
- She wants to work till 2 a.m.! Arrange a taxi to pick her up, or if you prefer go get her yourself, at least this once. Both options have a cost, either in terms of your sleep or your pocketbook. Both solutions, though, bring your daughter a little closer to financial independence and understanding the value of work. To my mind, that's worth some inconvenience.

OUR NOT-SO-DANGEROUS TIMES

Here are some numbers you are not likely to see in *USA Today*, *Time*, or hear about on Fox News. Criminologists Meda Chesney-Lind and Joanne Belknap take aim at the worriers among us who would tell us our kids are all bad, dangerous, and out-of-control. Things are simply not like that. If we were to take a city like San Francisco, and compare two seventeen-year-old girls, one from the baby-boom generation of the 1960s and 1970s, another, her daughter growing up today, we would find that the girl growing up now is much safer, much better behaved, and much more responsible than her mother was! The numbers tell us so. A girl is 50 per cent less likely to be murdered, 60 per cent less likely to be in an accident causing death, 75 per cent less likely to commit suicide, 55 per cent less likely to become a mother herself, 60 per cent less likely to commit murder, and 40 per cent less likely to be arrested for property crimes.[30] All this despite a media hyped on telling us that girls are all up to no good. The same results hold for communities across North America.

Try as we may, we just can't find much evidence that our kids are more at risk today than a generation ago. Instead what we are seeing is what is called "up-criming," a phenomenon where our children are more likely than ever before to be charged and tried for adult offences that would have been seen as nothing more than children misbehaving twenty years ago. Bullying on the playground? Parents might have been called, but these days the police become involved. The result is that the *incorrigible* youth has become the *delinquent*. It's the same for the truant child. We now think of that child as *conduct disordered* and seek psychiatric care. Suddenly just being a kid has become a punishable offence or a sign of deeper disturbance.

Oddly, it was my generation and the ones before me who were the truly violent ones, and for whom life was far more risky. We didn't have peer mediation in our schools to resolve interpersonal conflict. We didn't have easy access to condoms to avoid pregnancy and disease. We didn't have public health centres accessible just to teens. We didn't have remedial education for children with learning disabilities. And we certainly didn't have the endless stream of prevention education courses routinely offered to our children to warn them away from smoking, drugs, and early unprotected sexual activity.

OWNING UP TO OUR SUCCESS

So what's really happening?

What should we as adults really be worried about when it comes to our children? Where are the risks today?

In most cases they are still the same risks we faced when we were young, except they are dressed up a little differently. Some, like HIV/AIDS, are certainly more deadly than we experienced. Others, like bullying and stealing are likely to be dealt with through harsher sanctions, more accountability, and a greater likelihood that our transgressions bring us before a judge. But make no mistake. A generation or two ago we had sexually transmitted diseases to worry about too. And bullying was just as common, though the police weren't likely to become involved in stopping it.

We already know that statistically the *most dangerous* place for our children is not on the streets, but in our homes, where the vast majority of sexual and physical assaults occur. Beyond our front doors we have been successful making some of our communities safer. Those of us living in middle class communities, with their planned suburbs, a large residential tax base, and recreational facilities, are truly fortunate. An endless number of community initiatives are doing our children much good: public health education, safer school programs, criminal record checks for coaches, foster homes, shelters for abused women and children, mentoring programs, healing circles, suicide-prevention initiatives. It's all been working, quietly, in the less sexy world of community medicine, public health, community policing, and inclusive education. We won't see any television shows glorifying these programs or gripping drama documenting the daily grind of the public nurse, social worker, or safety monitor. Their work is seldom as exciting as that of the emergency room doctor. That doesn't mean, however, they haven't been achieving collectively a success unheard of in human history.

Maybe it's because everything is so much *better* that we are so quick to see the problems that remain. Whose problem, then, is our children's risk-taking? When I hear the pundits spin their lies, it's very clear to me that the greatest risk our children face is our refusal to acknowledge the good news. I keep wondering, if we know what we are doing has been working, then why aren't we investing more in already well-proven strategies? Instead, we seem to run scared and continue to invest old ideas like locking kids up, punishing younger and younger children for lesser and lesser crimes, being seduced by the very profitable incarceration industrial complex that has convinced us we need more prisons, more boot camps, and harsher rules. All of this sucks valuable resources from the programs that really do work and the kids who really do need our help when their risk-taking behaviours endanger themselves and others.

The alarmists are telling us lies. I recently read in *Time* magazine that a study by researchers at the University of Buffalo found that the younger a child is when he has his first drink, the more likely he is to abuse alcohol as an adult. In fact, we are even told that the chances a child will become an alcoholic increases by 12 per cent for every year decrease in the age the child is at the time of his first drink. If that doesn't scare us into becoming prohibitionists, then nothing will.

But wait. What that small piece in *Time* doesn't tell us is whether children offered a glass of wine with a meal are at the same risk of becoming alcoholics as the sons and daughters of parents who never let their children try alcohol, who never teach their children about responsible drinking. It's those children of the overprotective parents, I suspect, who are more likely the ones out behind their schools drinking. It's those children who will use alcohol as a way to convince themselves they are in control of their own lives, which, by the way, we know is *exactly* the same way many of their parents behaved when they were younger.

That study, typical of many, is less than meaningless. It sows fear among parents and convinces them that there is a problem where none really exists. After all, there is no evidence that the French have higher rates of alcoholism even though their children start drinking at a much earlier age than children in North America.

WHEN OVERPROTECTION MAKES CHILDREN SICK

The situation gets even more ridiculous when we see our kids actually being made ill by our desire to keep them safe. We have slathered so much suntan lotion on our children that for the first time in years children are developing rickets, a disease related to a lack of Vitamin D, most easily acquired from exposure to sunlight.

Of course, Vitamin D is also in milk, but that too is being taken away from children in our mania to keep them healthy. There appears to be a lack of good common sense when it comes to anything that we even suspect might pose a risk.

Maybe it's time we all just relaxed a little.

A father recently told me, "If something happens to my kids, it isn't going to be because *I* wasn't watching!" But what if something *never happens* to his children? What if they just never quite encounter enough life to prepare them to launch on their own?

If we believed everything we read (and we do!), we'd be in a constant state of panic over the well-being of our children (which we are!).

Developmental psychologists have shown that children need to experience their world first-hand to grow, intellectually, socially, and emotionally. We need to provide experiences that are progressively more challenging. Just think about what happens when a child doesn't take enough risk in school, won't try to read a more difficult novel, won't stand up in front of her classmates and speak, won't try any number of different strategies to solve a math problem. We know that the children who are most risk-averse are also the worst learners.

But learning to love risk can't happen in the sanitized world of the classroom alone. The risk-taker is a personality type we must cultivate at home and in our communities, as well as at school.

Of course, risk-taking when tackling a math problem creatively is very different than risk-taking out on the playground and starting a snowball fight, especially when the school has forbidden them. But they're not as unconnected as we may think. In fact, in my clinical practice, the healthiest children come from families (and schools) with adults who are balanced in their concerns, who are aware of their children's needs, but model for them how to have a life of one's own, with ups and downs, risks and pleasures, challenges and failures.

Advantaged or disadvantaged, we need to ask what challenges we are leaving for our children to measure themselves by. When adventure becomes navigating the Internet, surviving a Disney ride, or hanging out at the mall, then what are we offering as a rite of passage? How will our children show us they are ready to be adults?

ONE AND THE SAME

Patrick, the "car thief" I introduced in Chapter 2, told me about the rush he felt driving underage, uninsured in a stolen vehicle. He told me about how much his friends respected him when he pulled tricks like that. He explained how he had dreams of becoming a stockcar driver, like the racers his father had taken him to see out at the speedway one Sunday afternoon. He talked about the girls who thought he was "so cool" because he did things that pissed off adults. Because I listened and showed I understood that his stealing cars made sense to him, he was even willing, just for a moment, to admit that his chances of making it at school, of doing well enough to get a good-paying job, were pretty small. He knew he was headed for a life as a labourer, or if he was real lucky, maybe a deckhand on his uncle's boat.

Stealing cars and running from the police wasn't risk-taking behaviour to Patrick. It was an absolutely certain way to fight back the sense of failure he knew was waiting for him at the end of every school day. To his mind, the bigger risk he faced was to admit his life was going nowhere and ask his teachers for more help.

It was quite a different story for a fourteen-year-old girl named Robyn who was practically dragged into my office. "Rebellious" and "angry," at least according to her parents, Robyn had her own story to tell. Unlike Patrick, Robyn had no worries about failing out of school. She had done exactly what her teachers and parents expected her to do. At least until she hit puberty. Then suddenly the game of "Do as you are told" just didn't feel as satisfying. Her world, which had been so secure, became a world of caution signs, filled with people who annoyed her when they told her over and over, "Don't do that." So she did what any sensible teen would do. She rebelled. At least that was how her parents described Robyn's behaviour. I have usually found that when we label a child "rebellious," we are using a polite way of blaming the child when the blame should be equally shared with those who have been responsible for making the child's world too constraining to meet her developmental needs. Robyn's world of "dos" and "don'ts" may have fit the younger version of the girl, but it was failing miserably to meet the needs of a growing adolescent with a swelling libido, self-doubts, and a need to try being an adult.

What choice did Robyn have except to disregard her family, her church, test the limits of whatever values she picked up along the way. Her parents, in their panic, were so worried about what could happen to their little girl they never heard Robyn's plea to help her become a young woman. At a time when Robyn was saying, "I'm ready to take on much more," and desiring a smorgasbord of opportunities to act older, more mature, and more in control of her life, her parents were taking items off the menu, worried that Robyn was going to make mistakes.

REALITY CHECK

Despite the evidence, I will concede that all is not perfect in our hometowns. As much as we have reduced the risks our children face, we have also presented them with some new dangers we didn't encounter when we were young.

The most noticeable of these is our lack of a collective sense of community. I began this chapter by saying my parents put me outside in the morning and told me to "go play." What they had going for them was the assurance that on my little lower-middle-class street in the 'burbs there were ten other children bundled into snowsuits who had been put outside as well. And my mother was not just watching me from her living-room window, she was also quite willing to keep an eye on the neighbour's children as well. When something went wrong she was as quick to tell them to "Stop!" as she was to tell her own brood.

Some of our communities still look like that, but smaller families, more parents working, and the creeping tendency to structure everything for children means there aren't children out there for my kids to play with. And, very likely, there isn't a community of parents (mostly mothers at that time) to keep an eye on everyone's kids.

These changes put our children at some risk, for certain, but it is a risk of neglect, not a risk of attack.

Ironically, parents who want to overprotect their children often become so frustrated that they wash their hands altogether of their children's problems when their children stop listening to them. It is as if these children become excommunicated from what they most need: love and attachment. They are also the most vulnerable, ill prepared for either adventure or responsibility. No one has coached them along the way, preparing them for their independence. When things do get too out of control, these children may find themselves told by their parents, "Fine, you want to be responsible for yourself, be responsible," and a door slammed in their faces.

> *When we provide children with both structure and respect, balanced by a realistic assessment of the risks they face and what they can handle, then children get everything they need to grow up well: permission to mess up, and the structure to land softly after making mistakes.*

Sadly, these are also the parents who most often resort to David and Phyllis York's immensely popular *ToughLove* approach to parenting troubled kids. I often feel, though, as if they have read only the first half of the original 1982 book. They've got the "tough" part down pat, but they forgot the "love" part. A parent will tell his child, if you break curfew one more time you'll come home to a locked door. The child breaks curfew and "There!" the door is locked, promptly at midnight. Even the child's plaintive appeals for leniency don't sway these folks. And they shouldn't.

But those same parents are neglectful unless they also make arrangements for the child to sleep somewhere else. That's the love part of the *ToughLove* approach. It's up to us adults to make sure that the risks our children encounter are manageable. I hear stories of children breaking windows when locked out. And well they might. But a child with a reasonably safe alternative will get the message their behaviour is unacceptable and usually choose to slink off to wherever they are supposed to go. They may even cover their embarrassment with a little bravado, shouting, "You haven't won! I'm happy not to have to sleep in your stinking house." In my experience, they seldom mean it. When these children know they're loved and parents have modelled what it means to be responsible to yourself and others, children tend to get the message.

FROM LISTENING TO UNDERSTANDING

It's easy to see why we are left wondering why some children and teenagers act with such senseless disregard for themselves and others. If we are to understand their choices, then we will first have to hear what children have to say. This means:

- We will need to understand the importance of parents and other caregivers, not just peers, to children who live dangerously.
- We will need to provide a viable substitute for problem behaviours that bring troubled children powerful identities as something other than "problem kids."
- We will need to invite home children's street personality (and the peers who support them) in order to better understand who our children become and the risk-taking behaviours that make sense to them when they are out beyond our front doors.

Despite our best intentions, adults will not be able to influence how troubled children behave until we appreciate that what we call problem behaviours are, sadly, our children's pathways to resilience.

• 7 •

SPEAKING IN WAYS
RISK-TAKERS CAN HEAR

I supervised a nineteen-year-old counsellor named Mark at a youth camp where I worked years ago. What made him stand out from the rest of the young men and women I was there to mentor was that he was an accomplished rock climber who used to think it fun to climb the stone chimney of the main lodge, a forty-foot ascent that he did without a top-rope. I shudder to think what would have happened if he had slipped. To call him "impulsive" or "crazy," though, misses the point. To say he was driven to test his limits would be more telling. To say he wanted to get noticed and identify himself as different from everyone else might be an even more insightful way to appreciate what was a reckless act that could have, but didn't, get him fired.

There have always been young people like this, ready to scare us with their displays of bravado and downright stupidity. And yet, what have we offered young people as an alternative?

My father-in-law's brother loves to tell us stories of his life as a boy growing up in the country. Of his getting his first pair of shoes at age nine, of how far he walked to school, and of all the mischief he got into. One day, over coffee, I told him a little about Patrick, the teenager who stole the car and "accidentally" killed the father of three. The old man became pensive, then looked down at his feet. He shook his head in that dismissive way that those who have lived long do when they hear stories of younger folks twisting themselves into knots over the simple truths that they cannot see. Then he raised his eyes and looked me square in the face. "I guess if we'd had cars we'd have done the same," he told me defiantly. "Probably would have turned out just as badly too. When I was his age a bunch of us boys would take horses and run them through the streets. I once even walked a mare right into the schoolhouse, just to annoy the teacher. Oh, we were some bad, let me tell you."

And they were. For that matter, so was I. My generation caused our elders to fret with underage drinking, though nobody seemed to worry much about us driving under the influence. We watched kung fu films and then went out to the garage and connected two pieces of black dowelling by chain and called them nunchuks. In shop class we made metal death stars so sharp that you could throw them at a wall and have them stick. We were dangerous and everyone agreed that something had to be done. Parents met, laws were passed, and schools expelled the worst of the mischief-makers. Isn't it odd that each generation thinks they are better than the one that comes after them?

Such a short-sighted and self-righteous point of view is not going to help us to understand or change our children's risk-taking behaviours.

OPENING COMMUNICATION

Research begs us to consider that the right parenting style, and the right amount of risk, is going to be different for different children. What this means is that we are going to have to show some flexibility in how we communicate with our children. We are going to have to understand the broader context in which they live and the challenges they face.

Oddly, I find that it is often the parents who are the most beaten down who are the ones most ready to really *listen* to what their children have to say about why they take the risks they do. Children, too, seem most generous with their attention when parents are at their most vulnerable. Perhaps it is the shame they feel when they see their mother's and father's heads hung low, eyes teary, cheeks flushed with embarrassment, and hands wrung with anxiety. At moments like that, children seem more ready to drop the pretence of bravado and share their genuine thoughts and feelings. Perhaps they sense that their parents are more ready to listen as well.

That's how it was for Karl and his adoptive parents. Karl's dad is a member of that select group of parents who are professional law enforcement officers unlucky enough to have a child who messes up publicly. Anthony and Pat, Karl's parents, hadn't imagined things would ever get as bad as they did when they adopted their son at the age of three. They thought they'd done everything right. They'd read the books, went to church, purposely moved to a smaller town to be away from big-city problems. Anthony was home much more than most parents. Pat worked part-time. Karl had two younger siblings, both natural children. Both seemed well-adjusted.

At fifteen, Karl appeared headed towards a life of crime, though had so far miraculously been able to stay out of the "copshop," his word for his dad's police detachment. Both Anthony and Pat knew it would only be a matter of time. I worked with Karl and his family for more than a year, but really, Anthony and Pat did most of the work. They never believed their son was bad, and that made a world of difference to the kinds of conversations we could have. They kept at the relationship. They kept offering Karl time with them, and when he refused that, they offered him time with his friends in activities Anthony and Pat chose. Anthony took time to coach Karl's baseball team. Pat actually enjoyed playing taxi on Friday nights to get Karl and his friends to the movies.

But the drug paraphernalia still appeared in Karl's room, hidden in conspicuous places. There were the late-night phone calls, and then the evenings he would disappear for hours. One of Anthony's colleagues brought Karl home one night after finding him passed out drunk in a park. It wasn't a big enough town to keep these kinds of problems quiet, and word was getting around about the "cop's son." Soon there was a rash of break-and-enters, and Karl's name came up over and over again as a possible suspect. Several of his friends were eventually charged and jailed, but somehow the dragnet that trapped many of Karl's offending peers overlooked him.

It wasn't because Anthony attempted to influence the outcome. We would learn in time that Karl was not quite the delinquent he was made out to be. Anthony and Pat, though, put their foot down. Karl had to see a counsellor or, they feared, he was going to spend time in jail the next time he "screwed up." Karl could see the sense in this. He chose me over possible jail time.

What he actually got, though, were two doting parents trying to help and a little space each week for them to all talk about their relationship together.

"I don't understand. Is there something we can do to help you?" was what Anthony kept saying to his son.

Karl sat there, moody, rolling his eyes, one leg relaxed across one knee, hands folded. He'd shrug. I'm not sure Karl knew how to answer the question even if he wanted to. The question was too open, too vague. With some encouragement Anthony tried again.

"I'm a bit surprised, really. They're mostly good kids you're hanging around with. But they get into trouble. Actually, to tell you the truth, I can't quite figure how it is you haven't gotten into *more* serious stuff yet. You're almost sixteen, and some of them have already been in custody two or three times."

Pat jumped in, "We don't want you in jail. That's why we keep trying to help."

Anthony looked at his wife, then interrupted. "That's just what I can't figure, you don't seem to be getting into as much trouble as the other kids. Why not?"

It was that *difference* that stood out. Anthony's question was a wonderful door opener for his son. Karl perked up. "I'm not *stupid*, you know. It's not like I'm gonna go choose to be in jail," he said with a frankness that surprised us all.

It was a good, albeit rocky, start. "I think that's what's caught your dad and mom's attention, Karl, that you haven't been getting into as much trouble as they might expect," I said.

I caught Pat wanting to jump in, but she held back, wisely choosing to open some space for Karl to speak. We had agreed before we met with Karl that since we outnumbered him, we would have to work hard at making sure he had equal air time.

"I'm not trying to go to jail, you know. I'm just doing what every-one else is doing. It's not a big deal."

"It is when your father's friends drag you home drunk out of your mind," Pat threw in, unable to restrain herself any longer.

Children will become defensive under circumstances where they feel they aren't being heard. They will happily take more risks rather than have themselves become the scapegoat for their parents' worries.

"Like they didn't have to, did they? If they didn't want to they could've just taken me down to the copshop like they do to everyone else."

"I think your parents are glad they got you home safe that night," I said. "I'm hearing that they're worried about you, Karl, not really angry. That's what these meetings are about. To talk about these things, calmly." I hoped my words could get us back on course. It's so easy for conversations like this to deteriorate into everyone blaming each other.

"We're glad you got home that night, one way or the other," said Anthony. "Even looking the way you did. But we were talking about how you've managed to keep from getting into more trouble with your friends. That's what I want to know more about."

"Well, no surprise, really. I'm a cop's son. Think about it," Karl said, sarcasm dripping from his every word. "Like that night with the booze was a mistake. That's the only time it's happened like that, right? And you already know about the drugs. But, like, it's no big deal. I'm not into harder stuff, I don't even get into cars when every-one's drinking. *I'm not crazy.* I don't want to end up on the side of the road with my brains oozing out. I know what happens. I hear you talking about it all the time."

A faint smile passed across Anthony's face. It was matched by Karl. Pat looked confused.

"Sounds to me like Karl has been paying attention to some of what he's heard at home," I said. Pat stared at me, then at her son, and sighed. She wanted to believe what I had just said but was too wracked with worry to be sure.

I decided to leave the family to work things out on their own for a bit. I left and they stayed in my office a while longer. When I checked back they were chatting amicably, talking about stopping for some food on the way home. Karl said he was okay with that as long as they didn't eat anywhere his friends might see him. It was nice to see a "normal" parent-teen exchange. After all, we've all been fifteen.

Just because children are behaving in ways that look like high-risk behaviour does not mean that one child is in as much trouble as the next.

RESPECTFUL CONVERSATIONS

The kind of conversation Karl and his parents had helps a child like Karl explain his risk-taking behaviour to his parents in a way that makes the child seem . . . well, almost reasonable. Such conversations can help convince parents that their children are not the looney-tunes they suspected, but children on a mission to find something to say about themselves. Their penchant for danger is offset only by their equally passionate pursuit of recognition as an adult in training.

Anthony was successful getting Karl to talk because he looked for what was *different* about his son: ". . . you don't seem to be getting into as much trouble as the other kids" was the first step to making the rest of the conversation work. Through his words, Anthony conveyed to his son that he saw him as an individual, and responsible for what he was doing. That's not a bad place to start if we are going to come to an understanding of our children's risk-taking behaviour.

Once we started listening closely, we could all see that there was something about Karl that made him different from his peers. All children, even those who place themselves seriously at risk, usually have some limits that they impose on their behaviour. I rarely meet children, in jail or on the streets, who won't share with me details of some self-imposed limit on what they will and will not do.

If we go back through Karl's conversation with his parents, we find clues to its success:

- Anthony assumed Karl was different from his peers.
- Pat showed she wanted the best for her son and still wished to have a close, protective relationship.
- My role as counsellor was the same role a good family friend or relative could play, creating a safe place for the child and the family to speak and be heard.
- Anthony and Pat recognized that not all of Karl's friends were getting into trouble.
- Karl was given an opportunity to tell his parents how much he is like them.
- Everyone's feelings and worries were heard.
- Karl did not get blamed for making his parents feel bad.
- Karl's parents were sincere in their wish to help and it showed.

Youth who get help distinguishing themselves from their peers are given an invaluable lesson in how to define themselves successfully as individuals. Put a child on the defensive, however, and all he will do is argue how much like his friends he is or wants to be.

SUBSTITUTION AS INTERVENTION

My conversation with Karl and his family is typical of many I have with distraught families. I do everything I can to promote tolerance for children's problematic decisions that they say help them survive the challenges of growing up. Nothing I do encourages dangerous behaviour, though much of what I do does acknowledge that sometimes, for some children, *playing at being bad* is the only choice they have to make themselves feel powerful.

When we understand how risk-taking can be an effective solution to life's problems, then we are that much closer to offering our children an alternative that trades in the same currency of respect, responsibility, and influence. If risk-taking is a child's way of asserting his or her place in their community, then our alternative must offer a child an equal place. As much as I wanted to believe otherwise, children have taught me over the years that their behaviour is seldom changed permanently when adults like me try to coerce them into acting the way I want them to act. Children change only when there are advantages to changing that bring as many rewards as the behaviours that they keep repeating (being aggressive, abusing drugs, truancy, belligerence, running away, etc.). A child's behaviour, good or bad, is after all always a *search for health.*

I've learned it is far better to *substitute* than *suppress.*

Youth tell me they more often run *towards* something powerful and sustaining than *away from* that which threatens their well-being. If we are going to stop problem behaviour in our homes, classrooms, on our playgrounds, and in our communities, we are going to have to

Parents need to seek ways to offer children alternatives to dangerous, delinquent, deviant, and disordered behaviour. Alternatives must, however, offer the same quality of experience that the child achieved through his or her problem behaviour.

trade them conventional but *powerful* opportunities for risk-taking and responsibility-seeking for their unconventional and destructive sources of strength.

THE PROBLEM OF DEFINING PROBLEMS

The French linguist Jacques Derrida[31] had an interesting way to explain the odd manner in which our children challenge our notion that dangerous, delinquent, deviant, and disordered behaviour may not be all bad after all. Derrida talked about the way the words we use in and of themselves mean nothing. They are just sounds. Grunts and hoots. It is through collective conversations over time that these words become invested with meaning. But in this game of "name that behaviour" it's those with the power to decide what something means who are the ones who usually wind up making the association for us between a sign (a word like *rebellious*) and what it signifies (bad behaviour).

In this game of match the sign to experience, youth are sorely disadvantaged. Seldom are the ways they talk about their lives given much value by us as adults. A rebel, for example, may not be so bad if with the name comes the mystique of James Dean, the forthrightness of Jim Carrey, and the wild ways of Madonna. When we tell our children to "stay in school" or "be good," our advice is seldom heard in the ways we mean it. Children don't associate words like *school* and *good* with the same meaning adults have for these words. Therein lies the problem and the root of our breakdown in communication.

WHAT CHILDREN HEAR

Benignly, we adults approach children, inviting them to talk to us about their lives. All too often they resist our invitations. So many parents tell me that even when they approach their children with forthright questions and an earnest desire to listen, it still feels like their children close down. Many a parent has come to me for advice, as if somehow I had a magic wand that could make their children speak.

If only it were so!

Instead I have to rely on some simple rules of engagement. Here are some examples of what parents and other caregivers say, and what a child who is already angry might hear. A child who has a better relationship with these adults is likely to be less critical, more forgiving.

What we say:
I want the best for you. I want you to be happy.
What the child hears:
I want you to conform, to be just like me. Being happy is living like I do. What's wrong with that? Let me show you how to do things my way.

What we say:
I will try to give you whatever you want. Just tell me what you need.
What the child hears:
You need me. You can't get what you need on your own. You are still dependent on me.

What we say:

I'd like to get to know your friends better. Please bring them around sometime.

What the child hears:

I want to see what you and your friends are doing that takes you away from our home. Come home more so I can feel useful, a part of your life, and give you advice about your choice of friends.

What we say:

School is important. So is going on to college or university. You have to pay attention to your studies. Don't you see that?

What the child hears:

You have to grow up and work just like me. You have to have an education or else you won't amount to anything.

What we say:

Your body is your own body. You need to respect it and not let anyone tell you what to do with it that makes you feel uncomfortable.

What the child hears:

You have no sexuality. You couldn't possibly handle an intimate relationship. You should wait until you are an adult like me to express yourself sexually. Your body may be yours, but I still want control over what you do with it.

Admittedly, adults are not going to like the way children hear what we have to say. "Damn it all," we insist, "I have the kid's best interest at heart! If I don't say *those* things, what should I say?" The problem is that each of the above adults' statements needs to be said. Each shows love, compassion, and the sincere desire to guide children into adulthood. And each can be helpful when the child really believes the adult means well. However, when there is tension in these relationships, a different way of expressing ourselves is going to be needed.

Getting a conversation going with our children is easier when we recognize their need to take risks and the advantages they get from doing so. For example:

What we say:

It means a lot to me when you are happy. What makes you happy? What about your life is *working for you*?

What the child hears:

I'm comfortable expressing myself. I want to understand your world and how it works. I want to avoid judgment. I don't really know much about your life. *I need you to tell me how it works.*

What we say:

I know you have been good at finding what you need yourself. If there is anything that you need that you *still* can't find, please let me know and I'll help you get it.

What the child hears:

If you need me I'm here for you. Tell me how I can help. I know you are *competent* and can do things for yourself.

What we say:

What are your friends like? What about them has made you choose them as your friends? *Do you think I'd like them* if I met them?

What the child hears:

I want to hear about your friends and what in particular *you like about them.* I want to open up the possibility of meeting them, but *you can decide* if that's a good idea or not.

What we say:

School is important. So is going on to college or university. It's meant a lot in *my life* getting (or not getting) enough education. Do you have an idea of how going to school, or not going to school, is going to make a difference in *your life*?

What the child hears:

You are growing up and making decisions that have long-term consequences, like they did for me. I have given education a lot of thought and hope you do to. But I also want to understand *what education means to you.* Is it important? Will it make a difference in your life at all?

What we say:

Your body is your own body. It can have lots of different feelings. *It's all right to express these.* It's okay to have thoughts and feelings that are sexual. I hope you are able to find ways to express yourself *in ways that make you feel comfortable.* I also want you to know you can come and talk to me if something happens that makes you feel uncomfortable about your body or how others treat you.

What the child hears:

You have a sexuality. I know you will express that somehow. I want you to have a positive experience of those thoughts and feelings, and I'm there to help you if you get into trouble in your relationships.

NEW PERSPECTIVES NEED NEW LANGUAGE

It is not possible to do more than hint at what we can say to a child. Every situation begs new language. This book is as much about offering you a new perspective on children as it is a recipe book for helping them stay safe. With this perspective firmly in hand, I believe that whatever well-intentioned thing an adult says to a child will be helpful. In each of the second set of examples above, the adult does several things that make communication easier:

- Don't tell, share. The parent doesn't tell the child what to do, but instead offers to share information about the adult's life experience.
- Not knowing is a good place to start. The parent inquires with sincere interest about the child's life: what he or she likes and dislikes, feels, and thinks.

- Favour choice over advice. The parent leaves the choice for how the child behaves up to the child. It is unlikely the child will follow the adult's advice anyway, so why sacrifice the relationship for the sake of trying to be in control.
- Share from the heart. The parent owns his or her own feelings and thoughts, explaining what happened in his or her life and the consequences.
- Being there, now and forever. The parent offers to be there when the child wants to share things about his or her life, but the timing is up to the child.

ACTIONS SPEAK AS LOUD AS WORDS

It's one thing to tell our children, "Okay, I trust you. I believe you can handle things," it's another to show our confidence in their abilities to cope. I prefer to build bridges to opportunity for children and advise parents to do the same. A common principle applies, but each family will have to trust themselves to come up with the right amount of risk they want their child exposed to.

For a colleague of mine whose fourteen-year-old was refusing to go on a weekend visit to her grandmother's, the right amount of risk was not easy to discern. He and his wife could, they realized, leave their daughter at home, though they didn't feel very comfortable with that option. Nor did they want to force her to visit the cranky old lady either. Eventually, they decided they'd let their daughter convince them she could cope with a night by herself. This decision brought with it two perils. The first was that other kids might take advantage of her being alone to hold a party there. The second was that their daughter might get frightened late at night. Then what? They'd be at least three hours away by car.

The solution was to start slow. Though it took a lot more work leaving the girl than bringing her along, the opportunity gave her a taste of what she would be living in just a few years. "It's not enough that you simply tell your friends they can't come in," her parents cautioned her, "you have to be willing to call us, or the police if they get in and won't leave." That little bit of coaching seemed to work. Their daughter agreed and understood that there would be no second chance. There was to be no get-together in the house. Period. In the event of an emergency, or her deciding she just didn't like sleeping in the house alone all night, she could go to a neighbour's who'd agreed to leave a light on in the back and loaned her a key to let herself in. She could sleep in their sunroom if she wanted.

When we position ourselves as respectfully curious and appreciative of what a child is trying to accomplish by his or her behaviour, communication is most likely to flourish.

Before the parents left, they insisted their daughter parrot back all her instructions. That wasn't just for their benefit. They could see she was reassured by her answers, and probably felt more confident that she was capable of handling the challenge now that she knew what to do.

After they left, they phoned a few times too many, but in the end, everyone felt good about what happened. It was a calculated gamble. Not a huge step, but the kind of challenge the girl needed to experience to become comfortable with greater amounts of risk and responsibility. Far better, my colleague reasoned, to get it over with now at an age when his daughter was still more than willing to listen to what he and his wife had to say and put into practice their advice. When we speak like this with our children and offer them manageable opportunities to feel good about themselves, then we are well on our way to cultivating healthy risk-taking and responsibility-seeking behaviours in our naturally adventuresome children.

WHEN CHILDREN'S PROBLEMS ARE THEIR BEST SOLUTIONS

Occasionally, parents in the throes of crises misunderstand what their children are saying. More to the point, they wonder if rebellious children are just goading them with their questions and impertinence, or are they sincerely trying to understand their world? If we are to help our children grow up safe, to be wise in the ways of the world, then we must tolerate the way they express their growing understanding of their experience. In practice, this means that children's own stories of rebellion, philanthropy, desperation, or self-sufficiency isn't just a whitewash over what parents are certain is dangerous or disordered behaviour. These behaviours are the slow but steady evidence of a mind in development, making do with whatever is around to carve out an identity as someone worthy of note.

Granted, our children will drive us crazy with their behaviour. Far better, though, to be raising a child who is trying hard to figure out the world than one who readily accepts solutions handed them by others. Could it be that risk-taking and responsibility-seeking are a child's best survival strategy? Could all that noise and trouble really be in the child's best interest long-term?

I'd wondered about this for some time. Then, as I worked with more and more children, I kept hearing even very troubled youth tell me that they didn't think it's okay to do drugs, be abusive, drop out of school, or in any other way harm themselves or others. They know, as well as I, that being dangerous, delinquent, deviant, or disordered has its drawbacks. But they also know that in the absence of many choices, behaviours their parents perceive as stupid, or worse, reckless, are behaviours that make sense of the search for the four powerful messages that they belong, are trustworthy, responsible, and capable individuals. Their problem behaviours, they explain, are just rest stops on their way to adulthood.

Parents and every other concerned caregiver I've ever met worry that if we acknowledge the reasonableness of our children's problem behaviour, even for a moment, we may reinforce it. Take for example the fear that drives parents to oppose daycares for teenaged mothers and their children in high schools. "What if my girl sees those girls with their baby? It will make her want to have one as well!"

I'm not so sure. How did we ever come to believe that a child who has options would choose the chaotic life of the teenaged mother? Or for that matter, the delinquent, drug abuser, prostitute, or runaway? How can we doubt so much the common sense of our children?

Mind you, a teenaged girl will choose motherhood, or at least take risks that make motherhood more likely, when with the role of teenage mom comes a personal definition as a contributing part of her community or, at the very least, recognition as an adult. We know this to be true from more than thirty-five years of research with young women who tell us that when they are facing low grades at school, few job prospects, and little hope of ever escaping poverty, motherhood can be a way to jump to adulthood and assume a more powerful place in one's community.[32] Motherhood for these young women holds a certain attraction.

Not surprisingly, despite the apparent glamour attached to having a baby, the only girls I ever meet who have children they didn't want are those who got pregnant by accident. For those girls the role model of the teenaged mom at school is more likely a *deterrent* to unsafe sex that they tell me they should have heeded, a wake-up call to the consequences of what they were doing. Listening to those girls talk makes me think we should have daycares for teenaged moms in every high school.

Our children's behaviour makes more sense when we think back to our own childhoods. We too went searching for powerful ways to be known to others. For many of us, these expeditions in search of acceptance led us into strange places that our parents disapproved of just as much as we disapprove of our own children's behaviour today.

NEEDED: A NEW, MORE POWERFUL SELF-DEFINITION!

At some point during my career as a therapist, the kids won. I tried my darnedest to convince myself that *only some* risk-taking behaviours made sense, the ones *I* found acceptable. If I met a kid who drifted into drugs, or had a child while she was still just a child, I insisted to myself these kids were wrong, entirely wrong. Drugs cause more problems than they're worth. Same with teenage pregnancies. To be frank, I don't want kids doing drugs and I don't want children having children. I want kids to cope in ways that I approve of. Indeed, ways that I would cope if I were living their lives. I still hold these beliefs, only now I see they aren't very useful when it comes to counselling or parenting.

Instead, I'm coming to understand that different behaviour protects our children from harm in different situations. While drug abuse or an early pregnancy may be tragic, I've met youth who told me both problem behaviours saved them from feeling worthless, abused, unloved, or suicidal. I'd never have guessed that taking risks with their bodies and futures could be equated in their minds with survival. And yet, that is what they tell me. Their life stories show me that while some youth may not execute beautiful manoeuvres when it comes to dealing with life's stressors, they do keep pursuing success no matter the odds against them.

Expressions of our children's resilience may not suit us as their parents, but caution is needed when trying to change problem children. We need to first understand behaviour before we can offer a substitute that keeps children safe.

MANY EXPRESSIONS OF RESILIENCE

I've met children who rise far above their adversity in creative ways. In a Palestinian refugee camp I met boy scouts who welcomed me with a rousing collective pledge to protect their communities and nation. Where I come from nationalism is expressed much more quietly. For those children, though, it was an important way of asserting who they are and their hopes for their future. They taught me something that day about national pride and optimism.

A few days later in Israel, I met children who spoke of peace and ignored the danger that threatened them every day on buses, in cars, or while playing on the beach. Bombings, acts of terror and war, were so close, and yet children simply lived their lives, making friends and dreaming about their future. Those children taught me about persistence and the need to respect young people for their contributions.

In Pakistan, I've met seven-year-olds working in lightbulb factories. In Turkey, pre-pubescent girls work willingly hooking silk rugs, preparing for the day they will be good enough to be employed as weavers entirely in their own right. I can sit here in my North American home and wish child labour was not a necessity for these children, but it is important that I understand that the children themselves experience their lives in very different ways from what I imagine. In fact, research with children like these has shown us that children prefer to make a contribution to their families than to be a burden. They value the sense of responsibility that comes from their employment and how it makes others see them. Aid agencies are realizing this and no longer advocate a complete and immediate end to child labour. Rather they are now concentrating on a slow process of educating children and finding them a substitute, an equally meaningful role in their communities.

In a world of risk and contradiction, children follow the most unusual paths to health.

In Sierra Leone and urban America, children take up arms to protect themselves, either because of war, or the threat of gang violence. They are made to do unthinkably violent deeds to those they are convinced are their enemies by those who have much to gain by their hatred. By fourteen many of these children have known only war and violence and have lived an adult's life for several years. When aid organizations or the police come and decommission child soldiers and neighbourhood gang members, is it any surprise that these outside "do-gooders" meet resistance from the very children they mean to help? After all, what do we have to offer these children that they don't already have on their own terms? Power? Control? A sense of belonging? A meaningful role in their communities?

In the Far North, among aboriginal people, I've met eleven-year-olds who have gone truant from school to live on the land with their parents, forgoing the modern conveniences of television and central heating. These children, too, are fiercely proud of their language and culture even if they can barely read. Who are we, then, to say which path to resilience makes the most sense? It would seem the path children choose is always the one that, in one context or another, helps them survive and thrive.

PATHS TO RESILIENCE

What does it look like when a child saves himself from living with despair? Even the middle-class child from a wealthy Western nation is sometimes vulnerable to this despair. Children feel the nameless

dread of becoming just another part of the machine we call consumerism. Think Pink Floyd's anxiety over becoming "just another
brick in the wall" and you get the idea.

Odd really, that families who enjoy financial security and other
advantages, such as good schools and safe communities, still have
children who get into trouble, who insist on recklessly endangering
themselves. Ironically, wealthy communities can make greater
demands for conformity than low-income neighbourhoods. After all,
in those communities it's the mass-marketers who are the pushers,
not just the drug-dealers. As sociologist Henry Giroux has so elo-
quently explained, the corporate world is waging a war against youth
in which the only good kid is a kid who consumes.[33] Giroux worries
that we are making children into nothing more than commodities
that meet the needs of adults and the corporate elite, but for whom
we are willing to do little.

DIFFERENT COMMUNITIES, DIFFERENT SUBSTITUTIONS

Think about your community. Every community values something
different. Each wants to teach its children unique skills that will help
them to survive. What is it that your child should know how to do
that will help her become an adult and gain the rights and privileges
of adulthood in the community where you live? When we can
answer this question, we are better able to offer children a way
forward when they feel overly burdened. Not that children always
take us up on that offer! Sometimes they simply put our invitation in
the bank (their memory bank that is) and pull it out later when they
are a bit older and more ready to be a part of their community.

Each community, though, provides what a child needs to grow.
When I visited a kibbutz in Israel, I was impressed to find that children were given permission at age fourteen to move into their own
apartments a few hundred metres from the residences of their
parents. There, they were on their own a great deal of the time,
though still expected by the community to go to school, work part-
time on the kibbutz, and act according to what was expected of a
kibbutz member. It seemed to be working surprisingly well. I could

only laugh to think of children in my own community being given that kind of freedom. I also laughed to think how many parents would love to have a place to send their fourteen-year-olds!

But, of course, my children and my neighbour's children here in North America haven't been raised in a community where the boundaries between home and community are as blurred as on a kibbutz; where our neighbours' children are like our children's brothers and sisters. The entire lifestyle of the kibbutz prepares children for this early launch to this dependent independence.

I've met kids who prefer to become strongly religious members of their communities, surprising their more secular parents. I've also met children who want to revisit old traditions. I know a girl who learned to knit because that was what children used to do in the Eastern European culture of her great-aunt. She was equally interested in the modern artistic expressions of Eastern European culture such as the music coming out of former East Bloc countries. It all added up to an eclectic pastiche of colour and sound that she had used to create a lively personality for herself. It also drove her parents crazy wondering why their child was returning to roots they had long ago left behind.

Still other children will challenge us "old people" to look at traditions through new eyes. These are the kids who go to church with outlandish clothes, or learn to play the bagpipes of their Highland ancestors and then join rock bands, integrating bagpipes with electric guitars.

As strange as our children's ways of behaving may be, and strange they can be indeed, we need to remember they are never without purpose.

·8·

CONNECTING

F ar from being islands of independence, our children remain joined with us from their first breath well into their teenaged years. Risk-taking is nothing, after all, without someone to notice how exceptional we really are.

When my son was four he would sit and build towers with his wooden blocks for hours. He liked to build them up to precarious heights and then watch them tumble down. In his own little way, it was his rehearsal for bigger adventures to come. Sometimes, if successful at creating something extra-special, he'd call my wife and me to come and see what he'd done. He's older now, the blocks have been put away and new toys found. Now it's iPods and digital cameras. He's our family's official videographer, who puts together PowerPoint slideshows of our family vacations. The toys are different, their sophistication more complex than I often understand, but he still calls out to us to come see what he's made.

When we create a story for ourselves, we don't do it in a corner, off on our own. Though pop psychology has told us that we can create ourselves through isolated acts of self-reflection and personal growth, weekend retreats and classes in self-improvement, most serious investigators looking at how we create identity tell us that the individual only exists when others act like mirrors on our lives, reflecting back to us everything we need to know. Or how bad we are. Bon Jovi's song "Two Story Town" captures the desperation of youth who try to create new stories for themselves when their community and family insist on knowing them as nothing more than troublemakers. Many adults could sing the same lament. Most of us want to be known for *all* the stories we tell about ourselves, good, bad, and otherwise.

Do Something Different

Our children want us to notice them. When my son was tiny he wanted me to watch him play every soccer *practice* as well as every game. Now a teenager, he's too embarrassed to call me to watch him so he gets my attention in lots of other ways. He plays his drums extra loud and refuses to stop when I call him to dinner. He parades his friends through our house, descending on our fridge like a swarm of locusts. He's still very much letting us know he's there, even if it is in awkward, even at times annoying, ways.

Try this. For one week, look for examples of how your child is trying to keep you involved in his life, trying to tell you who he really is.

Think you're not important? Think again!

A friend of mine was doing her sixteen-year-old son's laundry and found a beer cap in his pocket. Coincidence? Maybe. Or was he trying to tell her that he's old enough to drink? Keep a little log book and pen in a pocket or somewhere handy in your house. Without saying anything to your child, pay attention to times he is doing things that might upset you, anger you, or bring your approval. Look for clues left like breadcrumbs in a forest. Even when our children don't mean to tell us about their lives, they do, and they are often happy to know we know more about them than we are letting on. When they stay out past their curfew, how do they let you know? What do they want to fight about, and do these pitched battles have anything to do with your child proving he's more grown-up than you think he is? When your child misses a meal, does he care if you notice?

It's our responsibility as parents to say something. Let our children know they are missed. My experience is that children prefer a reaction to being ignored. They want us to be concerned so they can throw our concern back at us, like an old pair of shoes they think they've outgrown but really still hold very dear.

If there is another concerned adult in the house, have them look for these same clues. At the end of the week compare notes. Talk with other parents about your observations. Then ask yourself, "Is all my child's dangerous and 'in-your-face' behaviour meant to keep me in his life?" You're likely to find you are much more important to your child than you think.

One caution, though. Don't share with your child your observations. If you do, you'll only embarrass him and make him feel self-conscious about how much he still needs you.

If you've read the clues correctly, you will be in a powerful position to build your relationship with your child. Try the following:

- Show your child he's impressed you. You don't have to approve of everything your child does. But you do have to make a big deal about having noticed. Ogle his outrageous dress and hair, then tell him what you really think. Comment how crazy he is to try the stunts he tries on his bike. Voicing your opinion doesn't mean disapproving. Talk about what you feel and think. *"I'd never be caught dead dressed like that!" "Watching you do those stunts made my stomach go woozy!"* These messages, conveying your experience of what the child is doing, without condemning him for doing it, tells the youth "You're still important to me, and I care enough about you to share with you what I'm thinking." I think of a child's outrageous behaviour as very loud communication. Like someone shouting at me. If they get my full attention the first time, they don't have to keep shouting, or do something even more risky.
- Do something, anything, to show your child you've noticed they are trying to be independent, more mature. If you catch your son drinking beer, and you've figured out it's his way to feel more grown-up, responsible, and trustworthy, then you might use the moment to talk about drinking responsibly. Talk about

your first drink, or even about times you've acted irresponsibly when drinking.

- Invite the young person to take on more responsibility around the house. To know what responsibility you should offer, read the child's clues like a fortune-teller's tea leaves. What do these clues tell you about what the child really wants? If the child wants more adventure, offer to be a part of the solution. Help him find it. Take him on an adventure, or provide the opportunity for the adventure and be there on the sidelines applauding.

A PLEASANT SURPRISE! OUR CHILDREN WANT US IN THEIR LIVES

In Chapter 5 I introduced fifteen-year-old Laura-lee who was doing what she could to take control of her life. All but raising herself, her parents seemed ambivalent whether they should be parenting her more or just washing their hands of her altogether. Though Laura-lee may be the poster child for the teen trying to make it on her own in many of the wrong ways, she had another story to tell, one that surprised me and gave me hope.

As Laura-lee and I built some trust in our relationship, she confided that for much of her life she had just wanted someone to *care enough about her well-being to tell her what to do.* It was an uncannily frank admission from a teenager who had created for herself the identity of the child who didn't need any help growing up.

"If you knew me when I was a lot younger, you'd have seen I always just wanted to be able to do whatever I wanted," she said.

"But not any more?" I asked one day when we had the chance to speak alone.

"No, like I still have power to make my own decisions. My mom's definitely not controlling me. I feel almost like an adult. Like responsible, it's not only responsible for others, but I'm in a way now responsible for myself too."

I had made the same mistake most adults make when they meet young people like Laura-lee. I'd inadvertently put Laura-lee on the defensive. I'd implied that the gig was up, that I knew she wanted to give up control of her life to someone. She had done what most kids do, thrown my assumptions right back in my face. She wasn't going to give up who she was nor the fun she had tackling responsibility and seeking adventure. I tried again. This time I asked, "Do you want that much control and responsibility over your life?" Not unexpectedly, her answer was different. I'd given her a way out, a way of saying, "Yes, but . . ."

She answered, "Well, not really. Having total control gets me in trouble, like with the police, with my dad, with the family. Because a lot of the stuff I do is illegal, or at least it's illegal for the people I'm with . . . It doesn't have to end up like that. It's just that the illegal stuff's exciting."

"Are you telling me it's better to have someone have some control over you in some ways?" I asked, trying hard to understand.

"In *most ways*, yeah." She laughed. "Like when I was doing really good was at my aunt and uncle's. My aunt was really strict with me and my uncle was laid back, which meant that it was really just my aunt being strict with me. I don't know, it just made me totally turn around. It was totally different from what happened at home."

"How so?"

"I'd just laugh at my mom. I didn't care what she said to me."

"But I don't get it, you wanted your aunt to take the control away from you?" I asked, still confused.

"I was mad at first, 'cause I still wanted to do what I wanted to do. Be with my friends, no curfew, out with my boyfriend whenever I pleased. But after a while, I don't know. I felt better about myself when she did that." Laura-lee looked every bit as puzzled as I had felt moments before. "When someone has control over me there's not as much that I can do. And the more stuff I can do, the more I tend to get in trouble. So when I can't do as much and I, like, have to divide up my time because I only have a certain amount of time to be out and with my friends, I know it sounds weird, but then I don't get into trouble. Not that I was getting into much before, but now it doesn't even look like I am."

"So giving up some control to your mom might actually make you feel better about yourself?"

"Yeah," she laughed again, louder this time. "But don't tell Mom I said that!"

GETTING NOTICED

It's no surprise then that many children steadfastly rely on a small number of people to repeatedly tell them who they are and what's so special about them. Some, in fact, have only one powerful way to describe themselves because those around them, including their parents, have offered them few opportunities to be anything else. Before our children turn to their peers, we need to remember that they would rather turn to us.

At least they would if we stopped treating them like incompetent, uncaring non-contributors to anyone's welfare but their own. In fact, according to a recent *Time* article about thirteen-year-olds, our kids hate being thought of this way. They resent being treated like "backstage adults," waiting to get onstage but not quite there yet.

We may want to hurry the process along. Remarkably, when *Time* polled 501 of these thirteen-year-olds, it found out how mainstream their values really are. Sixty-eight per cent thought that their parents have the right amount of involvement in their lives, and the vast majority practically mirror their parents' attitudes towards sex, marriage, and drugs.[34] Maybe it's just me, but these children seem ready to make a contribution.

Instead, many children, from both overprotective and undersupervised homes, are left on their own to find something to say about themselves. They tote around simple descriptions like "shy," "bully," "tough kid," "do-gooder," "geek," "always the responsible one," or just plain "crazy." We might look at these words and wonder why the child doesn't go in search of another slightly more pleasing self-description. But even these self-descriptions can bring a sense of security. The child knows who he or she is. The child knows the rules and how their behaviours help them get noticed, or remain invisible. The risks taken are always in support of the way they feel comfortable being known. As absurd as it might sound, the shy child might try suicide in order to become even more invisible. The bully will pick on other children if it gets him noticed by others on the playground. The crazy kid might just run around wielding a knife to convince everyone she is more messed up than anyone ever guessed. Even being "nuts" for some kids is an identity.

Other children are more adept at finding ways of being known to others. They pick up new ways of describing themselves like coins from a sidewalk. Whatever comes along is good enough for them. If doing drugs is a worthwhile pastime for one group of potential friends, then why not take drugs? If doing well at school brings with it a better, more widely accepted way of being known to others (and the child has the abilities to actually do well at school), then so be it. Children can be drifters between powerful identities as easily as they can be anchored to just one identity. Always, though, they are on the lookout for some way of hearing the four messages.

Some of the most strong-minded of children are able to carve out an identity without worrying quite so much if others will loan their support or not. These are the fortunate kids who insist we see them as unique and accept them on their own terms. I often think of them as the ones who shake up their churches with "Christian rock" or cause a stir at their schools by wearing something that no one else has ever worn. These are also the squeegee kids who walk down rows of idling cars at busy urban intersections offering to clean windshields for spare change. To hear them describe their work, they are "private entrepreneurs" making their own way in the world, not the panhandlers we mistake them for.

PARENTS CAN PROVIDE THE BUILDING BLOCKS FOR POWERFUL IDENTITIES

Though there are lots of people who play a role in our children's search for identity, children tell me they still look most to their parents and other caregivers like teachers to provide role models. If we are offering our own children a vocabulary with which to identify themselves, what words would they have that they would deem powerful and positive?

We all need recognition for what is unique and special about us. The most successful risk-takers are those that are adept at making those around them take notice of their talents. We know children's peers are more than willing to applaud many of the risk-taker's behaviours. But it is also our responsibility as parents to do the same. The more available we make ourselves, the less destructive the risk-taker needs to be to make an impression.

Parents are most helpful to children who thrive on risk when, according to the children themselves:

Children are on the hunt for new ways to describe themselves. As parents, we can provide them with powerful new identities or an endless stream of put-downs that tie them to old identities. The wise parent scatters in front of a child many different ways to be known as special. It is then the child's responsibility to choose.

1. Parents offer their children lots of different ways to describe themselves.
2. Parents invest lots of power in children's self-description by noticing what is special about each and every new identity the child experiments with.
3. Parents remain open to the unique combinations of identities that children put together. (Ever met a punk Christian? A high-school dropout with an entrepreneurial spirit?) These are often identities that combine something new with something old in order to create something powerful, widely accepted, and outlandishly unique.
4. Parents remember that they still have a role in their children's lives, no matter how "out there" their children's behaviour appears to be.
5. Parents help children find new audiences for whom children can perform their unique identities, people who will notice them and the special things they want to say about themselves. For example, it's important that parents tell grandparents about what children are doing, even when a child's behaviour is embarrassing. This is a sure way to keep children in relationships with their parents as it lets children know they are being noticed, even if the parents don't approve of their children's behaviour.

Do Something Different

Are you sure that your daughter's peers are pressuring your daughter to misbehave? Are you sure she got into trouble because she was told to do something she shouldn't have? Or could it be that your child, searching for something good to say about herself, has found a peer group that tells her what she wants to hear? How special she is. How grown-up she is.

Brainstorm all the messages your child hears from the people in her life. I like to draw in the centre of a piece of paper a stick figure to represent a child. Then I draw lines, connecting the child to all the significant individuals in her life (parents, teachers, extended family, bus drivers, friends, whomever). Next, put in quotation marks beside each person the most important message your child hears from them about her identity, good or bad. Do they call her a grrrl, a slut, a smart kid, a prep, a loser, a jock, a stoner, laid-back, happy, funny, trouble-maker, fool, or sexy? Now think about your child as a big piece of iron, and each message as a magnet. Which ones will she be most drawn towards? Who is going to have the most sway in her life? What is it about those messages that draws your child? Do those messages tell her she belongs, is trustworthy, responsible, and capable? Now consider, what do the messages you give her convey? Even if you are sending your daughter these same messages, ask yourself, why is she choosing to hear them from her peers or other adults rather than from her parents?

There's no easy answer to this last question. Every child is differ-ent, and changes year by year. However, if you discover that your child is not drawn to what you have to tell her about herself, you may want to try offering her a different message, one that meets her needs better. Here's how.

If you haven't recently, try asking your child:

- How does everyone else, other than her parents, see her?
- How does she want these other people to see her?
- How does she think you see her?

- How would she like you to see her? Older, younger, more mature, or less?

The messages children hear from us are expressed by both our words and deeds. If you want your child to be attracted to the messages she hears from you, you have to:

- *Say it.* Tell her powerful things about herself, things that *she* counts as important.
- *Do it.* Show her you think she can manage risk and act responsibly. Let her cook a meal for the family. Hold a part-time job. Ask to meet her boyfriend and make him feel welcome. Have that talk with her about birth control or abstinence that you've been putting off. Let her suffer some of the consequences for her actions (with you a safe distance behind to pick up the pieces if she needs help).
- *Love it.* Don't forget to tell her how much you love her, even if it feels a little embarrassing to actually say it, or for her to hear it.

TO GROW UP SAFE, WE NEED RELATIONSHIPS WITH ADULTS

"She's never at home any more. I'm lucky if I see her for two minutes while her nose is stuck in the fridge after school," complains Pauline, the mother of sixteen-year-old Marie. "Then she disappears. It's like having a boarder rather than a daughter." Pauline's complaint is a common one.

"My mom is always nagging at me," says Marie. "I just want to go see my friends, but it's always a big deal if I don't spend time with *her*. She really needs to get a life!"

It's a tough sell to convince parents who experience this scene that their children really still need them and are still very much connected to their families. For teens to feel powerful and self-assured outside their homes, they need to have as many relationships as possible across all spheres of their lives. This includes parents and other caregivers as well as peers.

Developmental psychologists are beginning to understand that people grow in connection with others. Marie would not need to

ADULT DECISIONS AND CHILDREN'S SURVIVAL

Our children are most at risk when problems get stacked one on top of the other. That can happen in any kind of family, one parent, or two, a gay couple raising children, or an extended family with the grandparents involved. There is scant evidence that one type of family, one way of living, is inherently better than another. Each simply provides different risks, including the lack of opportunities for adventure and responsibility that come with conformity.

We always need to ask, "Is our family's lifestyle a problem for the adults, the children, or both?" "Are the children up to the challenges we offer them?" and "Will anyone notice and applaud when they survive and thrive?"

Take for example an interesting telephone survey that Maeda Galinsky, a social work professor and researcher, did in 1998. Parents and children in families where both parents work were asked about their strategies to cope.

Far from causing insurmountable problems, Galinsky found that having both parents working presents children and their parents with challenges that can be overcome. I would argue that these children may even be the stronger because of it.

There are lots of ways that families can cope and stay connected despite their busy schedules!

- Get organized the night before so days start out in an orderly fashion.
- Set staggered wake-up times to decrease the morning rush.
- Create rituals to say goodbye and to say hello again later on, like walking to the bus together in the morning and cooking dinner together in the evening.
- Expect both children and adults to talk about their day. Encourage everyone to share their best and worst moments.
- Find trustworthy care providers and educators to supplement the attention of parents.
- Reserve some focused time to spend with the kids reading and game playing, as well as time to just hang out together.

> • Make sure parents have some time alone or with other adults.
>
> What these families teach us is that two working parents don't necessarily put their children any more at risk than a family with a stay-at-home parent (or for that matter one parent). In fact, children who have more responsibilities to contribute when parents are working are also children who are more on task, responsible, and see their lives as under their own control. Such children are also likely to tell me they feel a certain pride in the contribution they are making to their families. They feel important and competent. I think we may be worrying too much about our children when they are asked to contribute to their families. I say let our kids be exposed to some responsibility. It will do them good.

push her family away if there was space for her to drift alongside them. Unfortunately, we adults miss the obvious. The child is, after all, *still in our fridge, still eating our food, and still trying to annoy us more than anyone else!*

"For a child who needs me, she sure doesn't show it," Pauline tells me when I share this bit of news. "She comes in and barks some orders at me about what her Highness wants for dinner. That's if she graces us with her presence at all. And then when she does come home she is at us all night to stay off the phone. It's our friggin' phone!"

It's no surprise that it's difficult to see the relationship buried beneath all the conflict. But it's still there, if a bit battered and bruised. It's just that most teens show about as much grace as a bull in a china shop when handling the fragile feelings of those who raised them.

"RAISING PARENTS IS VERY DIFFICULT"

While as parents we delude ourselves into thinking we're the ones doing the "bringing up," our kids also spend a great deal of time dealing with our anxieties about their futures and about the risky situations they must put themselves in. To deny all this back-and-forth negotiation for control is to deny the essence of the strong relationship that is still there even as our children appear to be leaving the nest.

Samantha is very talented except she has no way to make those around her appreciate what is special about her. Her family values only the good grades she brings home in math and English. Those talents reinforce how they see the world. Middle-class business people with a strong entrepreneurial spirit, they want the best for their daughter. They insist she do something that will ensure she can support herself independently. No surprise, they find her artistic abilities frivolous, even threatening. Samantha tells me that to feel competent, she must also feel in control of the way her talent is looked at by others, especially her immediate and extended family. The biggest risks she takes are those that challenge what her parents believe about what she believes.

It is unlikely that everything a child needs to experience can be experienced at home or with one peer group. Children need lots of different experiences with lots of different people if they are going to decide for themselves what they value and believe.

Samantha would have been fortunate if she had encountered a school art program with a devoted teacher. But she didn't. That program had been cut for lack of funds. She may yet find her talent reawakens later in life, but for now it is quietly dormant, hidden beneath a restless aimlessness that pushes her further and further from those who love her. Some kids like Samantha draw (or trampoline, or play beach volleyball) despite what others think. But far more don't. Our job as parents is to root for our children and help them find what they do best. Often this means we must suspend our expectations and allow our children to lead. We have to give up some of our control to them. We have to admit we don't always know best.

TRUSTING OUR CHILDREN'S CHOICES

It has been ever thus. Irving Stone's fictionalized account of the life of Michelangelo Buonarroti, the creator of the David and the man who painted the Sistine Chapel at the Vatican in Rome, is aptly titled *The Agony and the Ecstasy*.[35] Stone tells us a story of an artist whose family could never understand his choice of vocation. The Buonarroti's were business people and it was into business that Michelangelo was to go. If ever there was a case for parents not understanding their child's talents, this was it. Samantha would do well to give the book a read. Maybe it would help her understand what she's feeling. After she's done, she could pass it on to her parents.

To feel competent children must have their talents valued by those around them.

We can only guess at what spurred Michelangelo on to such heights of creativity. To stand today among the throngs of tourists in the Vatican's Sistine Chapel and gaze up at the ceiling still evokes wonder at the vision and deftness of the eloquent execution of the murals. Thinking about what one sees, though, a benign God reaching down to humankind, Adam's hand so close to God's, and yet not quite touching, one might wonder if the painting is not a depiction of Michelangelo's own tortured relationship with his father. There is something timeless in the frustration we see pictured there. Many of us, like Michelangelo's Adam, are so close to connecting with those from whom we most desire admiration.

On the more mundane scale of our own lives, it can be just as frustrating for any parent to watch a child do what the parent perceives as risky. It is difficult to calm the fears of parents of children like Samantha who are certain their children's choices are putting them in jeopardy. In her parents' words, Samantha's desire to pursue a career in art would have done nothing except made her "starve." We cannot, however, decide for our children which talents are the best vehicles for them to achieve good feelings about themselves. We must allow them to be different from us, just as we hope and encourage them to be different from their peers.

We can make a difference when we create a world that has space for our children's choices. So many of our youth only find that space among their peers. It's time we looked to our youth themselves for answers regarding how to rescue them from meaningless lives or problem lifestyles that are their best, and at times only, solutions to the ennui of predictability and consumerism.

ANGRY SEPARATIONS

Angry teens, the ones most likely to be taking risks that endanger themselves and others, in particular, weave a complicated relationship with their parents.

When we fail in our role as cheerleaders, and become dictators over our children, we run the grave risk of pushing our children away and towards their more accommodating, and far more impulsive, peers.

Sean has lived much of his life in the dark shadow of his parents and the turbulent relationship he's had with them. Parent-child relationships do tend to get a bit complicated when a child like Sean burns his parents' house down while on a drinking binge with five friends, all under sixteen. Mind you, the problems didn't start there.

Before he burned down the house, Sean had been one of those teenagers who did little right. He existed like some subterranean creature in a corner of the basement, heavy metal posters adorning the cement walls. A battered stereo had stood in one corner, CDs in nice neat stacks contrasting with the one assigned novel and one school math book that both lay carelessly tossed open on the floor.

I had been in Sean's room on a home visit when I was working with Child Protection Services. Sean had been truant from school for a long time, and his parents seemed unable to get their son to attend school at all. They couldn't drag him. They had little or no way of punishing him. It's not like they were going to take away his things. He'd mostly bought them with his own money. He was too old to threaten, too old to bribe. If anyone was doing the threatening, it was Sean. On numerous occasions he had told his parents that if they tried to make him go to school, he would tear the house apart. He'd meant it, too.

It's not that Sean was a bad kid, necessarily. He was just struggling to do something with his life. He had never felt like he had many options, like he ever quite measured up. His father, ex-military, had been good at keeping Sean on the straight and narrow until he was thirteen or fourteen. Then World War Three broke out, or at least that's how Sean put it. "After that, the old man couldn't get me to do anything. He wouldn't hit me, but instead grounded me for months. I just laughed in his face. I'd sneak out my window at night, hang around with my buddies. Like I didn't give a shit. He could blow his rules out his ass."

I've met Ray, Sean's dad. Nice fellow. Really sincere in his wish to do the best for his kids. His other two boys, one older than Sean, one younger, are doing fine. But not Sean. Sean and Ray mix like oil and water. Whatever Ray was offering Sean by way of an identity wasn't sitting well with Sean. It was as if Sean was going to do anything he could to find something different to say about himself.

Sometimes, in a child's frantic search for a new identity, the child runs away from what he or she already has. This puts the child at great danger.

Ray took the news about his house remarkably well. He spent more time comforting his wife, Shirley, than showing what he must have been feeling towards his son. When we all met down at the jail where Sean was doing time, Ray was as supportive as he could be. Perhaps he just felt defeated. It was Shirley who couldn't stop asking Sean, "Why?" No matter what Sean did to explain the "accident," Shirley was never satisfied. She'd lost antiques, old photographs, knick-knacks collected over thirty years. It was as if her whole past had been destroyed.

Sean insisted the fire hadn't been planned. "We were all just skipping school. I remember going to the rec centre, hanging out there before the assholes told us to get lost. So we went to my friend's house. But his mom was home so no way. Then we went down to the liquor store and got this guy to buy us a bottle. My friend had snuck in and taken some money from his mom while she was upstairs. The weird thing was that we were just going to have a few drinks and save it for later, go back to the school and get our friends, then hang out." I was listening to all this even as Sean's parents sat, arms crossed, just waiting to yell and curse.

"Anyways, we ended up in my room, drinking, then when the booze ran out, I said what the f—, I'm already in major shit, so I went upstairs and broke the lock on the liquor cabinet. And I don't remember much after that, except for lying on the lawn while all the neighbours were screaming."

"Do you remember how the fire started? You told the judge one story, can you tell it to us again?" I asked, hoping a few more details might surface to help Shirley understand what had really happened.

"I think I was just fooling around. We had these pictures from magazines and were, like, burning holes in people's faces. Shit like that. Then somehow the drapes over my bed caught fire, and well, like, the flames were pretty. That's what we all thought. We were pretty wasted, right. But then, we were like, 'Oh shit, quick do something,' but by that point the whole f—ing ceiling was going up. I don't really remember much after that. Really. I guess I must have got out somehow," he said, looking straight at his mother, sarcasm dripping.

To her credit, even with the taunt, Shirley kept her cool, her eyes glistening with tears. Ray sat quietly, looking from the floor to his son, and back down again.

Eventually we would all work on some way to keep them together as a family. Sean realized with time that he hadn't found what he was looking for on the streets, nor with his friends, and he didn't enjoy being in jail. He insisted he wasn't a delinquent, just an angry kid who had harboured a grudge against his folks for the years they'd made him do things he didn't want to do.

A few weeks later I met with Sean alone. I knew his parents had been to see him.

"How are you doing?" I asked.

"Okay."

"Your parents, I heard they were in to see you. How's it going with them?"

"Better, really. Dad even looked me in the eyes last Sunday. I think it was the first time in months."

"Do your parents understand yet what happened?"

"Maybe, I don't know. Like, I've tried to tell them that probably over the period of years, just the hurt and pain and all that, I found it too much. I was doing a lot of dumb things. I don't think I deserve to be in here. It's not really a crime, well, it is a crime that I did, but I shouldn't be in here. It's different. I'm not really a criminal."

It's difficult to hear a youth like Sean minimize what he's done. He needs to be held accountable. "Maybe if you hadn't come to jail, you'd have never got the message, to stop all the crazy stuff. What do you think?" I asked him.

"Maybe," was all he'd say.

Sean thought he'd found what he needed among his peers. Those crazy afternoons spending time with friends appeared to offer him both the adventure and acceptance he craved. He was free to make his life what he wanted. He didn't have to listen to anyone. His friends appreciated him as someone who was more out of control than they were. In fact, with his friends, Sean could be the one person he could decide to be without his parents' permission: the delinquent.

SAFE AMIDST THE STORM

We know that we feel far less debilitated by feelings of helplessness and despair when others share our powerlessness. Alcoholics Anonymous and other similar groups have built a worldwide network of support based on this simple truth. People who feel the most burdened can provide each other a quality of support that others who are less burdened cannot. Should it surprise us then that groups of children who feel like they live outside the world of their parents turn to each other for some collective support?

There's been quite a bit of debate going on about who is really significant in children's lives. Psychological theories from forty and fifty years ago made it sound like the adults in children's lives were just a backdrop to a child's search for independence. Erik Erikson and Donald Winnicott, among others, convinced us that caregivers had specific functions to fulfill that, when done right, provided children with "good enough" parenting.[36] An adequate parent saw that a child's emotional needs were attended to. The child knew he could count on his caregiver to be there when he needed soothing. A parent was also supposed to provide a safe environment as well as one that met the child's basic needs for food, shelter, and clothing. When it all went well, poof, out popped a full-blown human being ready to work and love.

The loss of a parent, or less access to both parents, limits the options a child has to pick and choose a powerful identity from within the family structure. The solution is to look beyond the immediate family. Other adults in the child's community are good substitutes for parents when offering children identity choices and an appreciative audience for the child's performance of special things they want others to know about them.

I think parents' purpose is more than just fulfilling such basic functions. Otherwise why would kids, old and young, spend so much energy trying to get their parents to take notice of their behaviour?

Interestingly, if we look at some of the developments in the theory of family relationships discussed by feminist theorists like Jean Baker Miller[37] and Carol Gilligan,[38] who first presented their ideas in the mid-1970s, we get quite a different picture of parent-and-child relationships, one that explains why children want parents to notice and accept them when they take risks. Miller and Gilligan, and others like them, showed us how girls strive towards greater connections with those around them. Unlike earlier theorists who focused on children's search for independence, Miller and Gilligan found instead that girls move into progressively more complex relationships over time with more and more individuals having influence in their lives. In other words, they don't separate from their parents as much as increase the number of people they come to love. If parents feel less important to their teenaged daughters, it is because they move from being the only one of significance in the small, confined world of their child to just one among many influential people in the much larger world of their teenager. Samuel Osherson[39] built on some of these same ideas a decade later and found that this need for connection is as strong for boys as it is for girls. Spending any time at all with Sean and his family, one could not help but witness the deep emotional bonds between them, even as Sean played the delinquent and appeared to push Ray and Shirley away in favour of his friends.

THE U-TUBE THEORY OF LOVE AND CONNECTION

Most parents who find their way to my office, like Pauline, think of their children's capacity to love like a sealed U-tube half-filled with water as portrayed in the drawing below. To Pauline, it felt like Marie's emotional connection with her was diminished when Marie spent time with her friends. How could Pauline be of any influence on her daughter if her daughter appeared to be paying so little attention? In a U-tube, if the water goes up on one side, it must come down on the other. Sean's parents probably thought like this too.

Parents tell me, "My son never talks to me any more. All he wants to do is hang around with his friends." "My daughter hardly knows we're alive. She used to be such a nice kid."

The U-Tube Theory of a Child's Capacity to Love

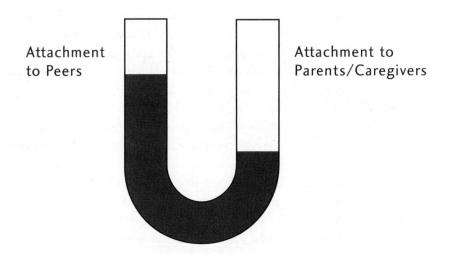

Attachment to Peers

Attachment to Parents/Caregivers

The Empty Glass Theory of a Child's Capacity to Love

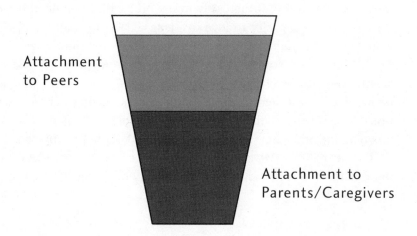

Attachment to Peers

Attachment to Parents/Caregivers

Do either of these laments sound familiar?

Contrary to what we think, kids don't experience their lives like that, any more than adults do. Our capacity to love is better described as a very tall glass like the one in the above illustration. A young child's capacity to love is minuscule compared to an adult's. Bit by bit, as the child grows, he fills the glass up. The more opportunities we have to learn how to love others, the fuller the glass. The fuller the glass, the more we are sustained and have people in our lives who can convince us we are worthy of respect and love. For as surely as we need water, we need love. But loving is a skill we need to learn.

We mistake the lack of day-to-day attention from our children, especially our teens, for the deeper attachment we think they have for their peers. But one attachment does not necessarily come at the expense of another. Each relationship, whether with a friend or a parent, adds more "water" to the glass.

SEPARATION? DIVORCE? DEATH OF A PARENT?

But what about when the love available to a child is split in two, made less available by separation and divorce, or is halved entirely by the death of a parent? Worse, what happens when a child is denied any love at all by parents who are battling over the spoils of a long-dead marriage? Where then does a child turn for the acceptance needed to say something special about himself?

Much has been made of the fact that children from sole parent homes tend to get into more trouble and are over-represented everywhere from mental health clinics to jails.[40] It's easy to blame the problems these children sometimes have on the absence of a parent, focussing on what is *not* there rather than what *is*. It's not fair, neither to the sole parent nor the child. Too often we forget that children have lots of people in their lives besides their parents, and that each is offering them an opportunity to define themselves in a unique way.

The U-tube approach to separation and divorce sees the child's world as "less." I prefer to be more optimistic. Children have shown me that they will keep filling up their "glass" with many different people and the variety of risk-taking and responsibility-seeking experiences each person makes available. The saying that "It takes a whole village to raise a child" is nowhere more true than for sole parents. Contrary to all the bad news about one-parent families, what I have observed is that when there is a separation, divorce, or death of a parent, there is more space in our nuclear families for others outside the family to offer a helping hand raising the children.

I've learned from children that there are many things a sole parent can do to ensure children turn out just fine:

1. Remind the child that they are still who they were before the separation, divorce, or death of a parent. Children can think that somehow they have changed inside when everything outside goes crazy.
2. Expand your reach. Help children make links to parent substitutes. These are the people who can mirror back to children the message "You are still okay!"

3. Encourage children to be with peers. Children will need friends who can provide a bridge between life before and life after the family crisis.

4. If standards of living drop, as they often do, find one thing that matters most to the child. If you can't afford it, come up with a strategy to get it, or a close substitute. Include the child in this plan.

5. Respect that children may idealize the absent parent. Remember, children look for recognition, and the haunting echoes that are heard from a parent that is no longer there can be powerful even if they are heard only in children's heads.

6. Let children see the sole parent's vulnerability. If we want kids to feel it's all right to express their emotions, we have to show them how we express ours.

Every situation will be different. This list could be added to many times over. The point behind all these suggestions is to recognize the strengths children have. By understanding that children will go looking for someone like a parent to offer them acceptance makes it easier to see why some children after the loss of a parent take even more risks, seek even more responsibility than they are ready to handle. Those behaviours are nothing less than their strategy to get noticed. We must never forget that no matter what our child's behaviour, in our children's minds, we still count a great deal.

Do Something Different

Think back to when you were growing up. As your world grew and you began to navigate your way to relationships with others beyond your front door, did you feel your love for your parents diminish? Or did you find that your love changed? Did your infatuation with a boy or girl mean you loved your parents any less? Or was it just that you had less time to spend with them? Looking back at your childhood, who taught you how to love others? Your father and mother? An aunt or grandparent? Where did you practise making someone else feel loved? Most people say their families taught them what they needed to know about how to love, but they got their best experience loving others in relationships with those outside their family.

Now think about your own child. Even if he no longer spends much time with you, ask yourself if you were really any different at his age?

Of course, if you need reassuring that your child still loves you, there's no shame in asking for it. Invite your child to spend some quality time with you.

- Take him out to a movie so he doesn't have to talk much. Just you and your son. No friends. Then, after the movie, keep the conversation focused on the movie itself. Avoid getting into heated debates. Avoid lecturing. Avoid prying.
- Take your child shopping. There are few kids who won't jump at the opportunity of a trip to the mall. Insist, though, that you spend some of that time shopping together.
- Offer to drive your child and his friends where they want to go. At least then he'll feel loved and you'll get to know him and his friends that much better. The more you feel a part of your child's world, the less you will feel abandoned.

•9•

,SLIM PICKINGS

Krista laughed at first when I asked her to bring along a few of her friends to our third meeting together at my office. She was eighteen at the time, and I was working with her to deal with her unbearable shyness. I had a feeling, however, that her few close friends had a better handle on what was going on with Krista than I did. Reluctantly, Krista agreed. The next time, she appeared with two close friends in tow, who sat on either side of her on my couch, as if defending her.

Krista was one of those kids who had matured physically much faster than her peers. By fourteen she was over six feet tall, with the kind of physical presence that gets noticed, especially by young men. She'd never been able to handle the attention. She was shy, awkward, mistrustful of the world in general, and men in particular. She struggled to name one, much less three things that she liked about herself, or felt she could do well. I coaxed and prodded, but still the list of strengths remained remarkably short.

Krista had reached out for help because she'd developed a pattern of drinking heavily, then allowing herself to be picked up by any guy who showed the least interest. She'd been so drunk during her last sexual experience that she couldn't quite remember the guy, or more importantly, if they'd used protection. The risky drinking and promiscuity, she explained, helped her cope with an incredible sense of embarrassment in most social situations, especially those where she'd meet boys her own age. She was embarrassed by her height, thought herself homely, and though she was in college, didn't know where she was going professionally or if she could even finish her year studying information technology.

Her family situation hadn't helped. For her two younger brothers and her, it was a constant battle to get any positive attention from their parents.

"My dad remarried last year," Krista told me. "I haven't seen my mom in years. My stepmom's a bitch. She keeps my dad from all his kids. And he's become real cheap. Used to be he'd give us whatever we needed, but now it's like he doesn't have any money when it comes to what we need. I just can't deal with my dad's new wife."

"What does your dad think of you, who you are, what you're doing with your life?" I said, trying to get the conversation away from what I knew I could do nothing about.

"He used to be a great dad. Real supportive, you know?" She paused, hot tears making her eyes moist, her cheeks flushed red. "But not much any more." Her voice cracked with the despair she'd been holding inside.

"If you say there's not much you think you can do well now, then maybe tell me about things you used to be good at, that your dad used to recognize."

She grabbed a tissue from the table in front of her, dabbed her eyes, and nodded vigorously. "There were lots of things. I used to get great marks, and Dad was always there at school concerts. You know, normal stuff like that. And I played basketball. And I had my friends. It was just like normal. That's all."

"And it's not like that any longer?"

"All of it's different, except the friends. I still have them." She shot a quick glance to either side of her, then looked down.

"What changed? It seems like you used to have lots of things you could do," I said.

"I don't know. It's . . . I guess I'm too shy now. The only time I'm not is when I'm in the bars and drunk, then I can come on to guys, really change, be happy."

In Krista's mind she had lost any reasonable way of controlling how others thought of her, especially her family who were still very important to her. She'd all but abandoned anything that made her stand out. Instead she was using alcohol and sexual encounters to assert herself. It was a feeble attempt to be something special and get someone to notice. That's how her friends could help. I hoped they would be able to tell me more about Krista than maybe Krista knew about herself.

Joey, a friendly university arts student, had been the first to introduce herself when she came into my office. I asked her, and Rosa, with whom she worked in a call centre, if they could tell me anything special about Krista.

"Sure," began Joey without hesitation. "She's very loyal and honest. She never backstabs or puts others down. And she handles the shit with her dad really well. I've met her stepmom. I know she's not making any of this up."

"And you, Rosa, what do you think?"

"Much the same. Krista never does anything bad except when she's drinking. It's, like, such a change then." Krista just looked down at her feet.

"Are you worried about her?"

"Yes," they both answered quickly.

"It sounds to me like your friends see lots of things to admire in you," I said to Krista. "But the bar thing's got them worried. What do you think would happen if you tried to just be yourself, stayed sober, and said hello to a guy?"

"I don't think I could do that," she replied hesitantly.

"She never does," said Rosa.

Joey looked at me. "I think you're right." She turned to Krista. "That's what you've got to start doing. You're meeting all these losers this way and something's gonna happen."

"What's Krista like when she's drunk?" I asked.

"She's very funny," Joey told me. "She's like she is when it's just us but she'll be that way with everyone. Lots of jokes, flirting, laughing, dancing, everything."

"But sober?"

"Dull, really. Quiet."

"I don't want to have to get drunk," Krista explained, looking more at her feet than her friends. "But that's been the only way. I even do that now at home. Last time we had the whole family over, I got really drunk on beer and started mouthing off to my dad." She giggled. "He was so surprised."

"Maybe you like the person you become when you're drunk," I said. "Sounds like you feel better about yourself, more in control when you're out of control."

I could see Krista was thinking about this. Her friends were too. When I saw she had digested that last comment, I asked, "Do you think you could ever be like that without the alcohol? Do you think you could ever have a conversation with your dad in a way that he got to know who you really are, all the special things about you, how outgoing you can really be, and assertive? I'll bet he hasn't met that part of you for years. Too bad, really, that only the guys in the bar get to meet that outgoing young woman."

"Maybe she should practise at the bar first," said Rosa.

It was not something I would have thought of. Then again, that's why Joey and Rosa were there, to help find ways for Krista to succeed that fit best with her and her lifestyle. Together, Joey and Rosa agreed to take Krista out one night and help her meet guys without drinking. They'd buy her all the pop she wanted, but she would have to stay sober.

It was a clever scheme, but it flopped. When I met Krista a week later, she told me she'd sat most of the evening in a dark corner, uncomfortably aware of being looked at by several men.

I suggested Krista practise being herself at home. After the bar episode, she was willing to try anything. Her friends, I thought, had had the right idea, only the wrong audience.

Fortunately, this time, the strategy worked. Krista had dinner with her immediate family the weekend following our meeting. She psyched herself up and stood her ground, giving herself permission to speak her mind politely, but assertively. She told me later that her father hadn't run away from her as she'd expected. In fact, he'd listened and even asked her to say more. Krista thought he'd been pleased that they were talking again. She said she felt much more powerful, and more like the mature young woman she is.

I hadn't really done much of anything, though it would have been easy to take the credit. I simply followed the lead of Krista's friends, helping Krista find experiences that brought her the sense of belonging, trust, respect, and competence she was seeking.

Do Something Different

If you think back to your own childhood, how many times were you right and your parents wrong? To some, that question may be heresy. But to be truthful, most of us can remember a time when we knew more than our parents. This doesn't mean our parents didn't have lots to offer us, only, they didn't know everything about what we needed, now did they?

Spend a few minutes right now and recall one time you were a better judge of a situation than your folks. How did that happen? How could you as a child have known more given your limited experience? Now carefully recall what information you had that they didn't. Then, ask yourself if your parents had realized how things really were for you, would they have given you permission to do something different?

We base our decisions on what we know. Can a forty-year-old really know what a twelve-year-old is experiencing?

Because we can't always know what our children need, we had better trust them to tell us, or at least be willing to try and convince us that what they are doing makes sense to them. It's easier to understand our kids when we:

- Hang out with them. Long car rides to and from concerts, ski hills, or even the library, can be an excellent time to hear what's going on.
- Keep the computer in a quiet but public space inside the home, not your child's room. If you are going to be a part of your child's life,

that means making sure you're seeing and hearing what he's doing.

- Talk about important things with your spouse or other adults in front of your kids. Remember, we are the role models for our children. If we show them how to respectfully communicate with one another about important things (that can be shared), then they are much more likely to come to us to discuss the dangers they face and the responsibilities they seek.
- The older your kids become, the more they will want to interact with you as a real person, with ups and downs, bad days and good. A child who feels he is respected enough to be trusted and confided in doesn't have to run to his friends to feel all grown up.

TRY THIS AT HOME

Translating what I do in a formal counselling session like the one with Krista into patterns of conversation that parents and caregivers can use themselves to help their children is not all that difficult. What can look like magic from the outside is in fact mostly about listening and forming a close relationship. Once I got to know Krista and how her risky behaviours make sense to her, it became obvious that what I needed to say was: "Maybe you like the person you become when you're drunk . . . Sounds like you feel better about yourself, more in control when you're out of control." Like any good counsellor, a parent too can reach this level of understanding with their children when they understand their children's behaviour as a search for the four messages. Danger is not always the problem we think it is. When we stop and really listen to youth like Krista, we find the clues to what they really want, and the substitutes we might provide them. Both are as close as their words. A parent who wants to nurture conversations like these can try the following:

1. See problems from the child's point of view.
2. Ask the child for solutions that fit her lifestyle best.
3. Be willing to compromise, or at the very least, swallow one's pride and acknowledge that the child may sometimes (often?) be right.

4. Invite others to help build the relationship back up. Friends, grandparents, neighbours, and professionals can be invaluable when relationships need fixing.
5. Never forget that, in most cases, the child wants a relationship with her parents as much as the parents want a relationship with the child.

It's important that we find ways back to our children when relationships go bad.

CHOICES AREN'T ALWAYS CHOICES

As Krista's story shows, the choices our children make to find others who will mirror back to them the four messages don't always turn out well. When a child's choices look downright crazy, it's most often because, from the child's point of view, options are few. What can look like pure insanity to those who watch over them, can be valiant efforts at survival. The worst situation occurs when misplaced efforts to find something powerful to say about themselves lead children into self-destructive pursuits.

That's what happened for teenagers Paul and Jason, who died when the stolen car they were driving went off the road during a high-speed police chase. A third youth, Patricia, survived the crash. Looking back, that "accident" was as inevitable as it was tragic.

I had worked for several years with all three, though I was on vacation when the accident happened. One evening, while visiting a childhood friend of mine in Montreal, my wife hesitantly read me the front-page headline over the phone and asked me if I'd known the kids? She thought I might. My tearful silence on the other end of the line betrayed the confidentiality I was sworn to keep. It would be several days before I got more details, but the weight of Paul's and Jason's death made all my work in the following months somehow more urgent. Patricia, the third youth, had walked away from the accident and went to jail, showing only emotional scars and a numbness that could be mistaken for self-pity.

These three had found among themselves and their peers a world

that made sense to them. They spent their days and nights present-
ing fortresses of invulnerability that encircled their fragile rootless
selves. The stolen car they were in the night they died was travelling
at twice the speed limit when it hit the
shoulder of the road and rolled, launch-
ing Jason through shattered glass and
crushing Paul. Only Patricia had made
the decision to wear her seat belt.

*Only when we understand how
risk-taking behaviours can
actually bring with them
acceptance are we in a position
to offer children an alternative.*

For most people who read the newspaper story it was probably just another
in a long list of front-page pieces about
kids who get into very serious trouble
hanging around with the wrong crowd. That's not what I read when I
finally saw the paper. For me it was a story of three youth who had
done everything they could to survive, creating the one powerful
identity they could find: "criminal." Together, they had helped each
other become the kind of out-of-control youth every law enforcement
and social service worker knows, and enjoyed a status shared by few
in their community.

Those kids lived fairly predictable lives. I've heard over the years
enough stories from kids like them, whose weekend escapades are
just as dangerous, to put the pieces together. Most likely, groups of
two and three would have begun to gather late in the afternoon.
Most of Paul, Jason, and Patricia's friends had stopped attending
school, so a Saturday-night party becomes less an excuse to unwind
than just one more evening in a long series of similar nights. Perhaps
part of the problem that evening was that all three had been out of
trouble for at least six months. They met in the parking lot of a small
downtown diner. They were going to buy some food, like any normal
bunch of kids, with money from their parents, who were happy they
were staying out of trouble.

But the real draw that evening was outside. The kids usually hung
out in the parking lot in front of the diner, and the management
didn't seem to mind as long as any fighting took place elsewhere. The
schoolyard up the street offered a perfect place to deal drugs. There
were back alleys to hide in, and as long as you weren't too rowdy

when the community police van rolled by, or cops on bikes stopped to chat, you could have a hassle-free evening. That night, the scene changed as it got later and little was happening. One of the youth knew someone who knew this guy in his thirties who said they could hang out at his house if the guys brought girls along. Eight or ten kids roamed up the street, the older kids stopping by the liquor store to buy whatever they could afford. Some others, the younger ones, would likely have brought with them pills, having saved up their week's supply of Ritalin.

Patricia explained, "One of the kids dealed so there was enough booze and softer stuff to last a while." Money wasn't tight among the kids so there was always enough to share. Only, after a while, they didn't want to stay at the man's house any longer. "He was like a f—ing creep. We didn't stay long." Patricia continued, "Once he started hitting on my friends, some of the guys started wailing on him and then we sort of left. I don't know what Paul did to him. I was already outside and gone."

Eventually the whole group moved back to the parking lot where everyone, a little more high, was ready to just hang out again.

The scene was getting boring by this point, though Patricia wouldn't admit it. From the autopsies, we know there hadn't been enough drugs or alcohol in either boy to get a good buzz going. Paul had suggested to the other two that they needed to get away for a while, go do something else, be somewhere else.

"Jason said he had friends we could crash with in South Bend, where he grew up. Paul said he wanted to go even farther, but like maybe we'd just get there tonight then keep going right across the country. Jason was keen, but I figured he'd be like no way once we actually had to do it. It was Paul's idea to steal a car."

Probably because it had been a while since they had been in jail, none of the three were apt to care if they did some more time in custody. I remember Paul telling me once that he didn't mind being inside at all. The food was decent, and he and his buddies got to build themselves up working out in the gym. Time inside was a time to dry out. And there was always the chance to meet some old friends. Besides, though Paul, Jason, and Patricia had maintained their residences while managing to skirt around most of the other conditions of their probation orders, they were fed up with just doing time outside. Really, when it came right down to it, there was no particular reason not to commit some crime. They had little or nothing to lose.

They went to look for a car. They started by just looking in windows of vehicles parked nearby, seeing what was inside, testing a few doors. Like most kids, they weren't motivated enough to choose a particular car to steal. They would just take whichever vehicle presented itself with an unlocked door. Eventually, there was a blue Honda with the window down, and the keys still in the ignition. A coat was on the back seat. The driver had gone in to pick up some pizza. It took but a second to hop in and drive away. The last car they had stolen had been driven out of town and burned. The next morning they had innocently hitched a ride home. This time, however, they scored eighty dollars in the jacket pocket and half a tank of gas. They decided to do the travelling they had talked about earlier. The police likely wouldn't be looking for them outside the city anyway.

Paul loved to drive. He refused to get his licence, though several of the youth workers who had supervised him had offered to help him prepare for the test. He could read, but had done so poorly over the years at school that taking any exam seemed like too much trouble. The other two youth would take turns driving later, but for now, all three were happy to just be moving. That was when they passed the police cruiser headed in the opposite direction.

It's hard to imagine that the police were able to make out Paul as the driver just then, but three kids in a blue Honda moving fast rang alarm bells. The police turned around and when they caught up to them, flashed their lights.

Having heard about these car chases several times, I know that the kids love the excitement. For Paul this was a great story in the making. Usually the youth end up telling their story in jail. In the retelling it is always the speed and the daring displayed by the kids that draws the biggest audience. Telling the story over and over not only passes the time inside, but also lets others know just how much of a risk-taker one is. I have no doubt that Patricia was right when she said Paul was having a great time driving fast, making like an outlaw. For certain, he would be thinking, "Here I am, one mean little f—er, outrunning the police." It would have been every teen movie-goer's dream, a virtual walk into the world of celluloid. It would have been better than a theme park. It was real.

"I knew we'd get caught. The police were like right there on our bumper. Don't believe that crap they said about pulling back. They were right there with us. I just knew Paul was going to ditch it, he was driving like a wild f—er," Patricia told me.

I think the chase was what they imagined they deserved. It would have fit better with their adrenalin-induced euphoria. It would have convinced them that they were dangerous enough to warrant the kind of attention they had seen on television. What the three didn't know that night was that to most of us who had tried to help them, their identities as criminals were nothing more than a fabrication. In our eyes they weren't the hardened criminals they imagined, but angry, confused children who needed us.

Seconds before the accident, Patricia told me she had shouted to the others, "Get your seat belts on boys, we're gonna crash." She had reached for hers and with that small gesture she had committed herself to living. Paul, the driver, died instantly. Jason wasn't so lucky. He was in intensive care for days as his parents and guardians help-lessly watched his slide into a death made bearable by drugs similar to many he had abused.

Maybe in that moment just before the crash, Paul and Jason found what they were looking for. Maybe just for that moment they were feeling on top of the world. Just for an instant, they were every-thing they wanted to be, they were right inside the story they liked to tell about themselves, living in a way that ensured them notoriety. They were invincible, untouchable. And in that spasm of excitement, the curve in the road would have been just another part of the ride. Only Patricia came out of the dream soon enough to get belted in. The screech of the wheels probably just added to the adrenalin rush for Paul and Jason.

I doubt when the car flipped that they worried much about anything or anyone, much less how they were going to land. I'm pretty sure that for Paul at least, his last thoughts were probably something like "f—ing amazing!" That was always how it was for all the other kids who'd survived, who came into treatment or custody after their "accidents." They never had regrets. Just what they considered a great story to tell. I might have believed them more if the way they spoke wasn't with such bravado. It was just too obvious that they were hiding from the pain of inadequacy.

According to children, the peer group they choose does not add to their problems, but instead is part of the solution to their problems.

As parents and caregivers, we have misunderstood the healthy aspects of time spent with peers. We've lost the opportunity to help youth build identities through their experiences with peers that can protect them against the personal, family, and community forces that threaten them. Does this mean that our children too will end up dead beside the road? In jail? Abusing drugs? Sexually exploited? The answer is an emphatic "No." A child's peer group, even a group riddled with "problem kids," has a significant role to play in supporting the health of youth, as does family, community, and the professional helpers who must sometimes become involved.

For most members of the community affected by Paul's and Jason's deaths, there would be the usual "tsk, tsk" as parents of other teens congratulated themselves on the fact that it wasn't their children in the car that night. Or there would be strained sighs of relief as other parents "touched wood," drawing upon their faith to preserve their own children, who, somehow, this time, had been spared.

The community and the social services system that served Paul and his friends held memorial services and reflected on what went "wrong." There is comfort in reassuring ourselves that what happened could have been prevented if those children had had "better homes," been in "diversion programs," had more "counselling," and certainly had not been hanging around with each other. But each of these salves on our collective conscience is not preventing these tragedies from occurring. That's because we need to understand better how these kids see their lives. We need to see that from the perspective of the kids themselves, many things went "right" for them that night.

Communities that work well for youth are ones that provide them opportunities to experience themselves as competent and the spaces to display those competencies in ways that the community both tolerates and appreciates.

COMMUNITY

There are other Pauls and Jasons in our communities who are looking for the right amount of risk in all the wrong ways. Our approach as a community of concerned parents has been to try and divert our children from troubled groups of peers, without understanding what it is that draws teens together and then puts them at risk of harming themselves or others. We ignore the fact that those groups are for some of our children their place of greatest strength.

Our ignorance causes us to overlook the more substantial problem of how our communities are leaving youth out. When we plan recreational facilities, when we design schools, when we create neighbourhoods that require cars to get around, how much have we taken into consideration the needs of our youngest members? Marc Zimmerman[41] and his colleagues have made the interesting observation that when communities provide opportunities for youth to be involved, through social action groups, church groups, or voluntary activities, children are much better protected from the risks they face. The greater their participation in the social and political life of a community, the less they have to pursue paths of resistance and deviance to get what they need.

It was a chilling lesson I learned when I met with the Palestinian youth I spoke of earlier. After talking to the youth about their plans for their future, which turned out to be a remarkable hodge-podge of goals typical of most children around the world, I asked their leaders about the violence that the children live with daily. I wanted, in particular, to understand how children were being recruited from the refugee camps and turned into suicide bombers. As you might imagine, it was a difficult conversation.

Remarkably, the adults I spoke with told me that sometimes children had to pick up stones and throw them at the soldiers who came into the camp in order to feel like participants in the political process. This was the children's only way to participate in the fight for their people's independence.

It is better to offer substitutes than suppress powerful identities among youth.

"The children who pick up the stones," I was told, "are not the ones we worry about. They feel they are participants, able to do something about the situation in the camps. *We worry more about the ones who don't pick up stones* [my italics]. They are the ones who get recruited. They are the ones who feel they have no voice."

Interestingly, the Israeli youth I met said much the same. Most did not want war. Most wanted simply to defend their territory, but not at the expense of doing violence to others. Their identity as an aggressor was one with which they felt very uncomfortable. Unfortunately, they too often felt powerless to oppose the more radical elements of their communities.

Though a world away from the streets of my community, I often think back to the children I've met overseas. They, like the children in my own community who feel they have few options for a successful future, are seldom heard when they speak. Children where I live also struggle to find a political voice.

When pickings are slim, children often turn to problem behaviours. These provide them a rock-solid audience, predictable in its enthusiastic support for their unique displays of dysfunction. These audiences also give children a forum in which to practise the role of risk-taker.

DANGEROUS TALENTS

The problem plaguing many youth is that we haven't let them have enough say over what is a sign of competence, and what is not. How are they going to show us what they are good at when what they are good at we don't value? We say to them, doing well at school is fine, but skateboarding is nothing to be proud of. They say, "But what about Tony Hawke, the world's most famous skateboarder?" We say being in organized sports is great, but we don't really have much admiration for the tough kid who gets into brawls. They say, "Is there really any difference between the brawler and hockey player Todd Bertuzzi's attack on his opponent Steve Moore and any other tough kid?" Of course, I don't want children to become swaggering streetwise delinquents (or hockey thugs). However, unless I acknowledge the potential power of our children's latent talents, I am likely to forget the magic behind the solutions kids find to tough situations. Furthermore, if I can't see their talents, how then am I to redirect youth towards socially responsible ways of expressing themselves?

Even our most dangerous children have talents. Our responsibility as parents is to offer children acceptable ways to express themselves that are every bit as powerful as our children's destructive alternatives.

To repeat the obvious, for our children to feel a sense of personal power:

1. They need to be able to *do* something that makes them special.
2. They need to be able to *reflect* on what they have done and realize themselves it was special.
3. They need to have *reflected back to them* by others that what they did makes them special.

Do Something Different

Who most noticed you when you were a kid? If you think of your choice of occupation, for example, who did you model your career on? Who inspired you, and how did they come into your life? Some of us were lucky. The people who became our role models were readily available. Many of us, though, had to go on a quest.

Draw a horizontal line dividing a blank piece of paper. Imagine this is your lifeline. Now beginning at the left, mark on that line the critical moments when your life took a turn for the better or worse. Begin at birth and continue until the present. Put the events that had a positive influence on you above the line, the negative ones below. How predictable has your life story been? Of those events that most influenced you, which were planned? Which were unplanned? A parent's illness, a sudden move, a chance encounter with a lover or friend, a job away from home, are all events that might have a profound and catalytic effect on one's life. Serendipity was for many of us a friendly ally in our search for identity.

Now think about your own child. What choices does she have? Are you as a parent doing everything you can to ensure that your child opens as many doors as possible? The more legitimate doors we encourage our children to walk through, the fewer dangerous, delinquent, deviant, and disordered ones they will find on their own.

There are more than four hundred occupations and twenty-five thousand jobs listed in government employment records. If someone were to compile a list of all the lifestyles open to our children, how long would that list be? They could become freeloaders, travellers, homebodies, entrepreneurs, home owners, renters, law-abiding citizens, criminals, hippies, consumers, volunteers, housewives, spinsters, clergy, unemployed, capitalists, socialists, night owls, or just regular Janes and Joes, whatever that might be.

You can help your kids make better informed choices by providing them opportunities to experience the world in much the same way you did, with both planned and unplanned encounters with those who are like them or different:

- Invite children to get-togethers where there are lots of adults. Don't be shy to invite them to house parties, funerals, weddings, or even office parties. These are places where they will meet people different from their parents and understand better the many different roles people play.

- Encourage children to job shadow someone they admire. At the very least, encourage them to come to your workplace for a day to see what the real world of work is all about.

- Don't make things too easy for them. If they need information about the latest computer game, have them talk to the store clerk, or call the technical assistance hotline. Help children develop the skills they need, and the risk-taker's attitude to put themselves out there when they need something.

- Listen to them when they tell you what they want to study during high school and afterwards. Remember, there is lots of time to experiment and take a few risks. People today are spending lifetimes as adult learners, most of us now experiencing seven or more careers before we retire. What's the rush? So what if a child takes a class in social studies rather than math? There's always next year to fix a "mistake." Meanwhile, the youth who studies what he wants to study won't regret having to go back to school for an extra year, nor is he the one likely to blame his parents for pushing him into becoming the science major he didn't want to become.

Lots of kids do things that they feel are accomplishments, but it's society at large that tells them whether what they've done merits being seen as a competent individual or a deeply disturbed troublemaker.

IN LOVE WITH CONFLICT

In the process of finding something special to say about themselves, our children grow up, challenge their parents, storm, resist, and, inevitably, adapt. That is, after all, what we'd expect. That's what we remember doing, isn't it?

In 1904, American psychologist G. Stanley Hall set out to convince us that all our suspicions about youth were true.[42] His work has had an enduring influence. Stephen Arnett,[43] a sociologist, writing a hundred years after Hall, tells us that our young people, especially American youth, routinely experience conflict with their parents and take more risks because of it.

Though we would like to think "storm and stress" is something kids have to go through, the truth is that's not the way it has to be. At least not when there are other choices.

In fact, many youth slide effortlessly through this middle period of development. Rather than demonize our children (and our own lives when we were adolescents), I'd rather accept teenagers' lives as a chaotic mix of reckless movement and tenacious holding to what is familiar and certain. Each child is simply doing what she needs to do to navigate a world that seldom provides a place for her to make a meaningful contribution. When choices are few, and expectations of our youth low, then kids get the message they should act like obnoxious teens. How else are they going to get noticed?

As parents, we can offer our children an audience as they perform something special about themselves. Problems arise, however, when we want to go backstage and assume the role of director. That's when our best intentions usually meet with rebellion or worse, the child abandoning his or her talent altogether. Best to remain an appreciative audience and watch and applaud the performance.

·10·

DECISIONS, DECISIONS

We need to work harder at finding substitutes for our children's behaviour rather than continuing to suppress behaviours of which we don't approve. We need to offer young people chances to make better decisions. We can increase the likelihood that they will take advantage of our offers if we begin to see the often invisible decisions they have made that distinguish them as individuals. It's these decisions to be different that are clues to how our children have navigated their way through the challenges they face growing up.

When I read case notes, or talk with parents of delinquent children, I'm as curious about what a child didn't do, as what he or she did. More than once I've found parents and teens staring at me incredulously as I ask them about those magic moments a teenager showed restraint. Yes, they may have gotten drunk, stolen a car, gone for a joyride with friends, had unprotected sex in the back seat, bought some drugs, and then driven out of town intending to light the car on fire. Even with all this confirmed, it is still important that we not assume the teen was acting just like everyone else.

In the case of one young man, Isaac, who did all of the above, I was impressed to find out that at a crucial moment, he had held himself and others back from becoming worse delinquents than they already were.

"I just didn't feel like doing the last part, burning it," he told me. "We'd had our fun, like I didn't care about that other stuff, but it was a nice car, and it just seemed really stupid to destroy it. I wanted to drop it off back a few blocks from where we got it. What were we going to do with a car anyway? Why trash it? The others weren't too happy about it, but by that point everyone was pretty tired so we just drove it out back of the mall. One of my buddies, and I won't say which, threw a rock through the windshield but that's all."

If we are to help children take risks that don't put them in more danger than they can handle, then we need to offer them ways to say they are special that prevent them having to throw themselves into decisions that are beyond their years to make.

Perhaps it's splitting hairs, but Isaac wanted me to appreciate what he had said and done that was a challenge to his friends and an assertion of who he really is. His parents, however, were fixed on talking about the rest of the evening. The police wanted to talk about stealing the car, the public health nurse about Isaac and his sexual activity. Everyone wanted to talk about what went wrong. If that is all we ask about, then our message to a child like Isaac is that he is stuck, permanently, being known to others in one way, and one way only. We will never find out other better things to say about Isaac and his pattern of risk-taking. It wasn't until I asked Isaac about his uniqueness that he told me a rich story about a boy who has moral limits. Rather than hearing from me, "You're a screw-up," my idea was to offer Isaac a better story to tell about himself. He seemed to appreciate the effort. He liked it that someone had noticed that he had made some good decisions for himself. My next job was to help Isaac find a better way to take risks. Where else could he find all that excitement and camaraderie?

Do Something Different

If you dare, ask your own parents how you behaved when you were the same age as your child is now. Were you a little hellion or did you dutifully obey your parents in every way they asked? Either way, ask yourself why you made the choices you did. Was it out of respect for your parents or fear? Maybe you were lucky and you never had to rebel or felt compromised by doing what was expected of you. Chances are though, how you were parented will exert a tremendous influence on how you parent your own child. Your decision to offer your child risk and responsibility is shaped by your own experience growing up.

Now consider, if your parents had to do it all over again, would they do anything different? In other words, what have they learned about parenting that you haven't? I'm amazed at the number of grandparents I meet who are far better at the business of parenting than they ever were when they were parents.

List on a piece of paper three decisions that your parents made for you that you wish they hadn't, three times they refused you an opportunity to experience some danger, some responsibility, that you craved and that to this day, you are certain may have helped you become a happier, healthier adult. This isn't meant to blame them. No parent is perfect.

Now, think about yourself as a parent. Is there one thing that thirty years from now your own child will say you denied her the opportunity to do? Write that down.

Help your child do that thing, but in a way that keeps her safe. For example:

- If your daughter wants to stay out past her curfew, insist she come up with a safety plan. If she can convince you that she will be safe, find a compromise that will let you both be happy.
- If your son wants to buy the latest video game rated Mature, and he's only twelve, check out the game yourself. If it's more violent than something you want him to be playing, say no. Then take him to play paintball, go waterskiing, snowboarding, or agree to purchase another game that you do approve of. (There are some great extreme sports titles that aren't nearly as violent as first-person shooter games.)

- If your daughter is sexually active and only fourteen, you'd be well-advised to see to it that she sees a public health nurse or your family doctor. If she's old enough to be making such risky decisions, then insist she act maturely and talk to a medical practitioner about the risks involved and the protection she'll need. If she's too embarrassed to talk about it, don't you be. Insist on discussing her choice and let her know you expect her to act responsibly even if you disagree with her decision.
- If your son insists on hitchhiking across the country and he's only sixteen, you may want to buy him a cell phone and a bus ticket just in case he decides otherwise. You might even insist he doesn't hitchhike, but then, how are you ever going to enforce your decision? Best to just bite the bullet and if you can afford it, give him the ticket. At the very least, you will know he is making a choice and can change his mind when he is ready to hop on a bus instead.

WHEN CHILDREN GET STUCK

What most puts Isaac at risk is how adults see him. He forever gets typecast as the villain. He's the Dark Lord of his school, destined to play his part in his personal drama each time he wants to get noticed. Isaac is typical of the repeat offender we see coming and going from jail whose only talent is getting into trouble. Or he can be the suicidal youth who is at a loss to cope with the stress of life and needs the constant support of others, either peers or professionals. He may also be the child whom we should worry about but don't because he is always playing the good kid and sacrificing his needs to the needs of others. The fragility of this *stuck* child remains invisible because he makes no demands on anyone, content to play his role.

Being stuck then, can mean:

1. Playing at being bad: showing everyone that the one way we know how to cope is by acting in ways that are powerfully *anti-social*
2. Playing at being good: hiding our vulnerability by *doing what everyone expects of us*, stuck always doing things for others

3. Playing at being ill: showing the world how hurt we are by *evoking attention from everyone around us for our weaknesses*, real and imagined
4. Playing at being invisible: *hiding* our depression, lack of connection to others, sadness, or anger. We ask nothing because we believe we are worth nothing. We hide behind shame.

Kids who choose one of these strategies tenaciously hold on to it. But repetition seldom brings resolution. The problems they had hoped to solve through their risk-taking and responsibility-seeking solutions only compound themselves unless something changes.

OUR FEAR OF YOUTH

Moral limits? Our crazed, out-of-control children distinguishing themselves from their peers? Subtle but substantial differences? It can all be a bit heady for the parent who sees before him a pierced, tattooed, mouthy teenager. My simple advice, don't judge a book by its cover. Far better to look at our children as pictures of themselves, a portrait they paint on the canvas of their relationships. Those motifs of resistance and self-expression are cues to our child's efforts at individuality. We overlook the uniqueness of their self-expression because we are outsiders to the culture in which it is displayed.

Sociologist Steven Miles talks about our children as a generation of scapegoats[44] – a generation of youth growing up with the fears of their caregivers forced upon them. The response must be to box them in, deny them self-expression in any manner except those deemed necessary by their overprotective parents. From where does this "ephebiphobia," a fear of youth, come from? Bernard Schissel, another sociologist who has studied youth, goes so far as to say we blame children for all our social ills.[45] They are the ones who are causing our cities to be dangerous and our morals to slide. But what have children really done that is so different from what we did? The answer is puzzling. The truth, or perhaps I should say, children's truth, remains obscured behind the misplaced nostalgia for a time in history when children were innocent and kind. The fact is that children have never been that different; we just idealize earlier times.

In the 1920s, the music was Dixieland,[46] there were dance hall parties and "rude" dances like the Charleston. There were slim-cut dresses for women and gang-inspired fedoras for men. It was a time of illegal alcohol and roll-your-own cigarettes. The Swing Kids took over in the 1940s, with jive and jitterbug, coiffed hairdos, and the GI Joe look. Then along came rock 'n' rollers in the 1950s with Elvis Presley and his swinging hips. There were high-school dances, drive-ins, and pool halls. The

Children practise making themselves unique and powerful in the eyes of others through small gestures. A wise parent notices their children's efforts and encourages them to be different, even from the parent himself.

Hippies took up the call for change in the 1960s, shouting their message through folk and acid rock, their experience of the music aided by legal and illegal mind-altering drugs. It was a time, we are told, of love-ins, rock concerts, and festivals. Then came the 1970s and along with the new decade we saw, of all things, disco and even stronger drugs like cocaine and heroine. Next it was the Punkers with their odd piercings, Mohawk haircuts, and lots of studded leather. More recently, the hip-hop kids have taken over with their edgy, and sometimes dangerous, street chic.

If we need to understand anything through this last century, it is that we have much in common with our children.

CONVERSATIONS ABOUT LIMITS

A conversation that helps a youth recognize himself as unique, with his own moral limits, must contain a healthy dose of curiosity on the part of the adult. We must be genuine in our desire to understand the young person's life. When that curiosity is not there, children rightly feel manipulated, as if somehow they are being worked around to saying the right thing.

But curiosity is not enough. We have to celebrate with our children that which makes the child stand out. In my experience, curiosity is easier to nurture than celebration. As parents we have our own sense of what is right and wrong. I never mislead a youth about what my moral limits are, and what I would accept as proper behaviour for *myself*. That's just good modelling. I may be curious about a child's world, but I hesitate to celebrate the young person's definition of morality unless that morality fits my own. When I can't, or won't, celebrate with a child what she believes, I can usually find something in her behaviour which is positive and which supports my Pollyanna view of the world as a place which is getting better.

We celebrate children's differences by finding something out of the ordinary to say about them. At some point all children assert limits on what they will and will not do. A wise parent celebrates her child's capacity to resist anyone (including the parent) who insists the child conform.

In practice this means I couldn't applaud Isaac's theft of the car, but I could heap praise on him for deciding not to trash it. His holding himself, and more importantly, his peers back from a wanton act of vandalism offered a glimmer of hope that somewhere inside Isaac there is a youth who respects the rights and property of others.

The noted Australian family therapist Michael White says helpers need to be curious about what is "absent but implicit."[47] Behind the stories we tell about the lives of troubled youth, there is often children's own dogged determination to take a stand against oppressive forces that would have them mindlessly conform. They want more. And so they should.

HIDDEN PATHWAYS THROUGH RISK TO ADVENTURE AND RESPONSIBILITY

Finding those special moments when children assert themselves as healthy risk-takers and responsibility-seekers takes patience. There is no easy path to understanding and appreciating the magic our children possess.

Take, for example, Asaf, a 265-pound, six-foot-one teenager in jail for assault and robbery, with a history of beating people up. He'd intimidate both staff and other residents by pounding his fists into cement walls, then walking around with a smug smile, his hand bleeding, the message loud and clear, "Don't mess with me."

It was difficult not to mess with a boy like Asaf. He was constantly getting himself into trouble at the treatment facility where I worked. One day, I encountered Asaf yet again threatening a younger resident. The boy wouldn't give up his seat in front of the television. I told Asaf to take another seat and left it at that.

A few hours later though the younger boy refused to participate in programming, saying he was afraid of what Asaf had threatened to do to him the next time he had an opportunity. I pulled Asaf aside to speak with him. I calmly let him know that we had heard he'd been threatening other youth again. I asked him to go to his room. Meanwhile, my co-worker was getting the other residents ready for their next activity. I told Asaf I didn't have time right at that moment to discuss his behaviour but would come and speak with him in a few minutes.

Asaf's room was eight large paces from us on the other side of a common room. He looked at me and my co-worker who stood a little way off, evidently frustrated and angry. He took eight heavy steps towards the door to his room. I watched him go and was just about to turn and get on with my other work when I saw Asaf tense. I wasn't expecting him to reconsider his decision. Then, in what seemed like slow motion, he turned to look back at me and with incredible force threw three punches at the two-inch solid wood door now unlocked in front of him. The whole room echoed with the thwacks. I was about to say something when I saw Asaf turn on his heels and take four steps back towards me. I remember all four. Each brought me closer to panic. I had no way to defend myself if he chose to harm me.

From across the room, my co-worker was watching. I could see him beginning to move in Asaf's direction, but he was too far away to do anything. My gaze turned fully on Asaf, who looked at me furiously. On his fourth step, Asaf's fists clenched at his side. He stopped. An immense wall of anger, he stood there for only a second, then turned and picked up a steel chair that was in easy reach, lifted it above his head, and threw it on the floor with such fury that it broke the industrial grade ceramic tile and mangled the chair. At that point, Asaf marched back to his room and slammed his door shut.

I kept my composure, just barely, phoned for backup in case Asaf reconsidered his retreat, and locked the boy's door. A little shaky, I went to the staff lounge and took a long break.

The next day, I spoke with Asaf. He'd been moved to a more secure holding cell for twenty-four hours of observation. I'd had some time to think, hug my own kids, talk with a colleague about what had happened. The question that nagged at me most was what made Asaf stop?

"Why did you mangle the chair, rather than me?" I asked him when we met the next day. "You've certainly done worse. What held you back?"

"It wasn't worth it. I don't feel like doing any more time in jail. And besides I didn't really want to hurt you. You never did anything bad to me."

I was both surprised and encouraged by what I heard. We would talk more about this incident, but at least for that moment, I was able to compliment Asaf on his decision not to hurt someone. He'd finally made a decision to try a different identity, one that would lead him towards a less violent life. In his own way, he'd taken the biggest risk of his teenaged years. He'd behaved differently.

SHOUT, THEN SHOUT LOUDER STILL

Teenagers insist we notice what's unique and different about them. If we don't they're forced to shout louder until we do pay attention. Green hair, studded dog collars, driving ambition, a parade of sexual partners, good marks in school or flunking out, athletic feats or risk-taking stupidity on bicycles and in stolen cars. These are all displays of individuality by teens that depend on relationships with others for their validation. The "mirror"-starved teen whose exploits receive little attention will keep on looking until he gets recognized. Teens tell me they search until the identity by which they want to be known is mirrored back to them by those they count as important. If that means, as the saying goes, "lookin' for love in all the wrong places," then so be it. Teenagers reason, "Better recognition from delinquents than no recognition at all."

But not everything different about a teen is worth mentioning. The trick for us seems to be to pay attention to the things teens most value. The more one gets to know what teenagers find important, the more likely we will be to notice the special things for which youth want to be noticed. To paraphrase the family therapist Steve de Shazar, it's all about finding the difference that "makes the difference."[48]

There are some differences that count more than others in shaping a child's life. It is up to parents to pay close attention to their children's talents and decisions if they are to help children see themselves as significantly different from their peers.

These differences inoculate our children from the *disease* of conformity, control, and criticism they experience when not accepted for who they are or want to be. These differences are nurtured through experiences of risk and responsibility. If we look closely and appreciate these differences when we see them, we can be reassured that our children can think and act for themselves.

To notice these differences, there are some places that might be more fruitful to look than others. Not every child is as complicated as Asaf. Not every one needs professional help. Talents are one of the most obvious places to start to find those differences that make the difference. What does our child do well? It may be obvious if you have had the resources to train them in piano or violin, speed skating or basketball. You might also rely on other adults in your child's life to fill in some of the gaps. How does she do at school? At a part-time job? When volunteering? Over at the neighbours? It needn't be a formal skill. Maybe your child is known as a good-hearted person who loves to talk with seniors. Maybe your teen is recognized by others as a great babysitter.

IN SEARCH OF GOOD THINGS TO SAY

Most kids have something good that can be said about them. A few make it more difficult for their parents. What we define as a talent and what a child considers an important skill may not be one and the same thing. After all, those talents that depend on risk-taking behaviours to be experienced may be ignored, or squashed, by parents worried for their child's safety.

If we mean well, and are genuinely curious to understand our children's lives on their terms, most children will give us the time and attention we need as adults to understand how they survive and thrive. Our children are willing to explain their lives when we adults are willing to listen with open minds.

This all becomes much clearer when we consider the experience of a youth like Chantal. Chantal was certainly different. She kept telling me stories about the occult rituals she had participated in, of the risks she'd taken, of how responsible she felt having chosen her religion herself.

"So you really know all those secret chants?" I asked her. "Do your friends tease you about being a witch?" Though I was trying hard to be curious and non-judgmental, to be truthful, I was actually a little repulsed by some of what I was hearing. Drinking blood, scarring, the strange dress codes. Still I try to keep my message clear and upbeat, as if saying, "I'm intrigued. And yes, you can be sure I know this behaviour of yours gets you noticed."

"Yeah. I don't talk too much about it 'cause it freaks some people out," Chantal told me, obviously pleased to have an attentive audience. "And I don't talk to my parents about it much either." Chantal even went so far as to tell me that she was not even supposed to tell me that she belonged to a group of Satanists nor that she had read "their bible." Somehow the group felt it had more power by keeping their activities secret.

"I can see why you wouldn't share this too much. It certainly could put some people off," I told her. "It's not what I believe, but there's something about this which is really important to you, isn't there?"

"Well, it's not like we kill children or cats or anything f— up like that. But what we do to worship is a whole lot better than that crap at church."

"What's different?" I asked, swallowing hard.

"Like first we don't force anyone to do anything. My mom's a

Mormon and she and all those other holy rollers make me sick. They're always trying to convert you. We don't care or think people should force each other to do things, but like just because we think something's evil doesn't mean it is. It's hard to explain."

I'm a hard sell on stuff like this. But still, I'll listen if that helps the child come around to a less oppositional relationship with me and others in her life. Though it might sound like I'm not challenging Chantal, there would be very little point to mentioning how some might find her words offensive. She was unlikely to hear what I had to say anyway. Besides, she'd already had plenty of experiences with adults who put her down.

In a pithy moment of insight, Chantal told me, "My mom doesn't respect my choice of religion but expects me to respect hers back. That's what's crazy."

The real threat to our children's well-being is not their outlandish displays of defiance, but blind compliance with what they are told to do. I prefer a child who thinks for herself over one that accepts the influence of the mass-marketing machine, who stages no act of resistance to cultural norms. It's these compliant youth who need their worlds disturbed, and made to exert themselves more in search of an identity.

MAKING KIDS SAFE FROM MASS MARKETERS

I'm actually less concerned about the child who takes an outrageous stand like Chantal's to prove she's different from other children and her parents than I am about young people who are mass marketer's dreams. Their expressions of themselves usually extend to "buying" an image, literally. That image is crafted for them on the front pages of glamour magazines or in store windows. They choose from the limited Fall or Spring collection, then find a way of being different by mixing and matching from what is already pre-selected. What worries me most about those teens is their lack of skill development, their reluctance to take risks or responsibility for themselves. They are the ones who buy the pre-ripped jeans, faded and torn, made to look grungy and hip, with $69.99 price tags. In many ways Chantal is learning far more than them about negotiating with the world for an identity. She's making it up herself. And yet, strangely, Chantal worries us more than the mall kids who appear to fit in.

Advertisers prey on our kids. A particular line of clothing gets pushed to the point where the child feels he or she has to afford it, or convince parents to buy it. With the purchase, we are told, comes instant status. It angers me that kids without financial resources are shut out from this popularity contest. Once again being acceptably hip becomes a commodity of the rich. I know the less well-off kids have the advantage of having to find their own look, but one still can't ignore how much harder this becomes when a youth feels her choices aren't choices at all, but symptoms of her marginalization.

What's left for those who can't afford to buy themselves a "look all their own" or the middle-class kid who doesn't look like the models on the magazine covers? What can they do to be just as powerful? Delinquency? Cheap diversions in the form of alcohol, or street fighting? Is it any wonder these children choose one of the 4Ds to hear the messages they need to hear when more conventional pathways to success seem blocked?

·11·

COMING HOME

Romeo: *By a name*
                    I know not how to tell thee who I am:
                    My name, dear saint, is hateful to myself.
                    Because it is an enemy to thee;
                    Had I it written, I would tear the word.
                    Shakespeare, *Romeo and Juliet*, Act II, Scene II

Poor Juliet. She chose to love a boy her family could not accept. He in turn had no choice but to hate himself for what was not his fault. It's been almost four hundred years since Shakespeare penned *Romeo and Juliet* and still parents are making the same mistake.

Like it or not, we are going to have to let our kids bring home the identities they forge beyond our front doors. If we want our children to avoid destructive behaviours, we have to offer them a safe place to be themselves, a place to proudly show us their risk-taking and responsibility-seeking selves.

That means putting aside our prejudices about their lifestyles and choices.

It means appreciating how well our children are doing. I am reminded of H.B. Gellatt's[49] theory of "positive uncertainty." Gellatt, a career and vocational counsellor, recommends that we accept the chaos that is life. We do better when we embrace instability and remain open to changing our future as opportunities present themselves. He tells us:

When we are open to hearing children explain their world to us, we encounter stories of survival and hope. Children may make "bad" decisions, but they rarely, if ever, make decisions that don't bring them feelings of competence and control.

1. Be focused and flexible in what you want
2. Be aware and wary about what you know
3. Be optimistic in what you believe
4. Be practical and magical in what you do

It may be difficult at times to see, but the children who survive best, despite the crazy ways they adapt, are the ones who demonstrate this flexible, optimistic, and creative approach to their problems. That adults often find their solutions incredibly difficult to accept does not change the fact that for many children, their high-risk solutions bring with them, at least temporarily, resolution of their problems. All those dangerous, delinquent, deviant, and disordered behaviours (the 4Ds) are chosen by our children when they can find no other way to be competent, caring contributors to their communities (the 4Cs we want them to be).

If we hope to help children keep themselves safe, we are going to have to appreciate better how what they do is often an expression of positive uncertainty. Their behaviour is proof of their commitment to finding some way, any way, to experience risk and responsibility that brings with it status as adult, and the right to direct their own lives.

Do Something Different

Consider the absolutely worst thing your child has ever done. If nothing comes to mind, or your child is still too young to have done anything to harm himself or anyone else, consider your greatest fear. What is the worst thing your child could do?

Now assuming your child did do something bad, ask yourself what benefit the child gets from behaving badly? Does he impress his peers? Does he feel like he belongs to a powerful group of individuals? Does he feel older? Does he get noticed in ways he values?

Next, consider what else he could have done, given his family background, the community in which he is growing up, and the talents he has? Was there really a better choice?

Finally, and this may be too painful to consider at all, ask yourself if you've offered a substitute for his problem behaviour. If you have, does that substitute give him everything that his problem behaviour brings him? Does it provide equally powerful versions of the four messages he wants to hear: "You belong," "You're trustworthy," "You're responsible," and "You're capable." If the answer to any of these questions is a resounding "No," then the problem you as a parent face is how to find another substitute.

If we want to let our badly behaved children know there are other more socially acceptable ways to meet their need for risk and responsibility, we are going to have to offer an apology, forgiveness, and then provide them an alternative: an apology for whatever we did that denied our children the opportunity to express themselves in our homes; forgiveness for the ways they have embarrassed and harmed us with their troubling behaviour; and an alternative that lets them hear the four messages from us, their parents. Be prepared for some tears, ours and theirs.

To find those alternatives:

- Be flexible: We will need to tolerate more noise, and more mess. We will need to accept that our home is not just a place for adults, but is equally shared with our growing children. They must have private places to express themselves. They must have their own keys. They must have choices about what they eat and when.
- Honour who you are: Our homes also remain a place for adults. While exercising flexibility, we can also ask for respect. We can ask for a time each week when we spend time together as a family. Eating together is an obvious solution (even if the menu is

planned by the kids). We can insist on quiet after certain hours and that the house remains free of things we find repulsive: pornography, drugs, or other items that undermine our values.

- Be optimistic: We need to convey to our children that we believe in them and show that optimism by letting them take more risks and responsibilities inside our homes. We do this by making our homes places children first learn to entertain others, talk back (without being degraded or physically abused), speak their mind on controversial issues, drink alcohol (it's a legal substance, after all), celebrate their special talents like skateboarding, rapping, or gaming, activities not usually applauded by adults anywhere else in their community.

- Be magical: Remember to have fun. Our children can be great companions. Invite them to play with us, but think of play from their point of view. If you like to cross-country ski, and your kids find it boring, switch to downhill or at least alternate activities week-to-week. If you like long Sunday walks in the park, what about breakfast at a local diner beforehand, then let them bring their bicycles to the park so they can tear around but still meet back every half hour? Maybe they want to spend all their time with their older boyfriend and no longer have time for you. An easy solution is to open your front door to him and find out what he's good at. Who knows, you may find you have a mechanic, a painter, or a computer technician at the ready and happy to help out around your home. The more you see the boy as a man, and your daughter as a responsible young woman, the more they are both likely to live up to those expectations whether under your supervision or not.

THE QUEST FOR A POWERFUL IDENTITY

Children find the oddest solutions to muddle their way out of identities that bring them nothing but put-downs and inconvenience, sadness and isolation.

We parents play an immensely important role in their search. Our homes are the very best place for them to practise the skills they will need to succeed beyond our front doors. Over the years I've seen much creativity expressed in this regard, but one of my favourite stories comes from a sixteen-year-old boy, Robert, and his stepfather, Martin. Though I'd never recommend their solution as a way to solve conflict between a parent and child, somehow, for these two, their unique, if not illegal, solution seemed to resolve some harrowing family dynamics. It also brought with it for Robert the kind of risk and responsibility he'd craved and found in even more troubling ways.

I had coached Martin and Robert to spend some time together to see if they could build a relationship. They had been in one shouting match after another for years and Robert's mother, Denise, was pleading with them both to find a way to be with each other peacefully.

Martin's solution was to take his sixteen-year-old stepson to the one place he felt he could talk with the boy "man-to-man" – a bar. Sitting there drinking beer all afternoon, Martin's view of his stepson changed. Whereas before he'd told me Robert was "nothing but a kid who doesn't deserve respect," after the boozing he was willing to concede the kid was "a little messed up, but otherwise okay."

I had naively thought they would go fishing, take in a ball game, or go out for coffee.

If Martin's change in opinion about his stepson was an unexpected surprise, Robert's changed view of Martin was just as curious.

"When you both went out and got drunk, what changed?" I asked Robert after Denise had called me and told me what had happened. She'd been just as taken aback at what Martin had done.

"Well, I noticed we could relate to each other when we were drinking. I guess we were getting along better," Robert told me. "We could communicate better. We could basically talk about anything. Usually if I tell him something he puts me down, but that changed. And I didn't put him down like I usually do either."

So what changed between a father and son? The question puzzled me. It wasn't just that Robert got a few free beer off his stepdad. Something else had caused a change in their attitudes towards one another. Robert said he thought Martin had finally recognized that he was a young man, not a boy who needed to be told what to do. In their world, a trip to a bar signalled a rite of passage for Robert. In some cultures these rites of passage might be a tad more spiritually grounding. But in Robert and Martin's world drinking with one's "old man" is one way to sanctify a boy's transition to adulthood.

I never underestimate the capacity of children and their families to find creative ways to solve problems.

It was a welcome change for everyone when Robert felt he had arrived at a more mature status in the eyes of those who loved him. He was a quiet and moody boy who dressed in the same long baggy pants and loose-fitting jacket every day. I worked with Robert and his family on and off for more than a year when it became clear that Robert would soon be either in jail, a detox centre, or a foster home if his behaviour didn't change dramatically. Just before we had started meeting, Denise had become so frustrated that she'd insisted Martin move out. This had pleased Robert and his behaviour improved. While he continued crashing most nights at a neighbour's house, he'd said he felt better about spending more time at home once Martin had left. Robert had even begun to look into returning to the school he'd been kicked out of months before.

But the separation between Denise and Martin was only brief and soon Martin began staying overnight again and tensions escalated in the home to the same level they had been before. That's when the family had sought counselling to see if there was any other way to help Martin and Robert get along better.

Martin meant well, but he had unrealistic expectations of his stepson. Martin was adamant that Robert could be an all-star hockey player and pushed the boy hard to be responsible and practise. This pressure came despite Robert's small stature and his dislike of team sports. To Robert, sports weren't his way to seek adventure or responsibility. To fight back, Robert did whatever he could to let Martin know he wasn't, and would never be, Robert's real dad. His behaviour in the community continued to be a problem, with it seeming like every social worker and police officer knew him by name.

MAKING AN ADULT FROM A CHILD

When we started meeting, Robert's parents saw him as anything but adult-like. They had been using lockouts and *ToughLove* measures to try and control Robert. All that had happened was he'd become more and more depressed and unresponsive. He kept blaming the problems in his life on Martin but was convinced no one was hearing what he was saying. Denise tried everything she could think of, but sadly, nothing she did had much success. Robert was going to change in his own good time.

If Robert's story at home was one of troublemaker, in the community among his peers, he held a different status altogether. There, he was the kind of kid who liked to take chances, but also kept others safe. He defended his friends fiercely. "We're just a bunch of kids trying to get through life, not a lot of bad kids like people think," he told his parents and me during one of our early meetings.

It was this peer group identity that had been his salvation, preventing him from becoming suicidal or seriously delinquent. Outside his home Robert was actually trying to be responsible for himself and others. "I don't really know what I'm good for, but there are things, I guess," Robert told me in his characteristically self-deprecating way. "I'm easy to talk to. That's what people say. I always help my friends out when they have problems, and I give good advice." Martin had never known this side of his stepson. All he'd ever seen was a good-for-nothing brat who caused trouble.

"Like, my parents think I'm not good for nothing. They just don't realize what I am good for. And they've never seen me being mature," Robert told me shortly after we'd first met.

"What's that mean, being mature?" I asked.

"Maturity is behaviour, just the way you act. I don't know the right words for it," he told me hesitantly. "Maybe, it's like how old you act? Like if someone is always hitting someone or wrestling in public then that's sort of immature, but if you are maybe at a ballet or something, you don't do that stuff because it's immature. But when you're with your friends, it's appropriate. I see myself as someone who is trying to prepare himself as an adult. I guess I want to be an adult even if I don't act like it all the time."

"How do your parents see you?"

"Right now I think my parents think I am a bum because I'm always getting into trouble. And I could have helped that by not getting into so much shit, but now it's too late and they've already started looking down on me. You know? It makes me feel like dirt. It almost makes me feel that they don't care about me. I know they do, but it makes me feel that they don't."

The concerned parent helps youth challenge the labels adults give them, while supporting youth's efforts to bring home the labels they construct among their peers.

Months later, without intending to, Martin's invitation to Robert to go for a drink would be the first time either parent had invited home the more mature identity Robert had created for himself on the street.

OPENING AND CLOSING THE FRONT DOOR

The best thing we can do for our children's mental health is invite them back into our homes. Their "street" identities are not the enemy, any more than their peers are. Trying to understand our children is a fruitless exercise unless we ask them to be our tour guides. If we think we already know what is and is not going to provide a powerful identity for our children, we are likely to be proven wrong.

An example may help to illustrate this point. Peacekeeping troops in Afghanistan were in danger of killing children who pointed guns at them. In most cases, these were guns that had been discarded because they no longer worked. The situation was causing the soldiers incredible amounts of worry as they were never quite sure how to respond. While all this is interesting, it was the solution that the peacekeepers found that teaches us something important about children.

The soldiers discovered that these children, raised amid the constant turmoil of war at their doorsteps, would happily swap their guns for pens. Once the word was out, children literally lined up to make the trade.

How to make sense of this strange solution to a dangerous situation? If we think about it from the perspective of children searching for a powerful identity, there is some rhyme and reason to all this. Having a gun in Afghanistan, where weapons are plentiful, may not bring with it the same cachet that having a weapon does for youth in the West. But a pen – that's different. That is something that really says something about you, something unique. Having one brings with it status as someone who attends school, is bright, a future leader. It is also something foreign, rare, something that says you are worldly and different from your peers.

THE DOOR TO UNDERSTANDING

In our children's hunt for the right messages about themselves, ones that bring respect and power, nothing is ever as it seems. If we are to understand what it is that draws our children into risk-taking behaviour, then we must try and understand the meaning of their behaviour to them. If we have any hope of ever helping them construct alternative stories as powerful as the ones they author with their peers, we need to be in a relationship with them that matters. We need to understand their world from their point of view. Their key back through our door is the acceptance we show them.

It all begins by sending cues to young people that they can come home and be themselves. Parents who send this message are likely to meet their children's other identities. But beware. As a consequence of these encounters, parents may become even more worried for their youngster's safety, or they may become much more confident in their child's capacity to solve her own problems.

It works like this. Some parents will suddenly know their son or daughter does drugs, sleeps around, skips school, or simply never eats the lunch they've packed for them. That's the worst-case scenario, that children become more forthright and honest about what their lives are really like outside their homes. There are other parents who will experience exactly the opposite. When their children come home with their street identities, parents encounter children who are far less deviant than they imagined. When parents take the time to listen, they may hear that their children are getting involved at the local recreation centre and doing so well at school it's embarrassing, or are the ones who, among their peers, keeps everyone else safe.

Do Something Different

Whatever your reaction to the street identity your child brings home, take three breaths and talk to someone *other than your child* about it. Remember, you asked for it. All those sleepless nights spent worrying aren't going to keep your child any safer. Now that you really know who your child is, you're in a much better position to help her act safely and responsibly.

- Get yourself some support. Find another parent who is coping with the same problem behaviours. Laugh, cry, spit, stomp your feet, curse – do whatever it takes to cope with your feelings. But don't dump them on your child. Not if you want your kid to still be there in the morning.
- Develop a strategy. Find a way to say to your child, "I'm concerned about you," and "I love you." Find a way to offer what the child needs to stay safe. Your child's sexually active? An *open* box of condoms in the bathroom is a wise investment (if the box is open, one being taken is less likely to be noticed). Not comfortable with that, get over it! If your child is already sexually active, you have no choice but to follow the youngster's lead. Keep talking and offering alternatives, including a visit to your family doctor or a public health nurse, but in the meantime, keep your child safe.
- If things get out of hand, seek counselling. There are lots of fine counsellors available. Bodies like the Canadian Counselling Association (www.ccacc.ca) and the Canadian division of the American Association for Marriage and Family Therapy (www.aamft.org) can offer links to qualified clinicians in your community. The yellow pages can also help. But don't forget your child's guidance

counsellor or your church clergy, rabbi, or imam. The child who brings home her identity is likely to be the child who is open to seeking counselling with her parents. I prefer family counselling to individual work with children. Family counselling doesn't make the child the problem. Children are much more likely to participate in counselling when they don't feel like they're the scapegoat.

LIMITS TO WHAT WE ACCEPT

This is not to say parents and other caregivers must accept everything their child brings home or into the classroom. Kids' street identities can be like stray cats or dogs that hang around our front porch for a few days, hungry and alone. We have to coax them inside if we want to keep them, but we also don't accept them unconditionally. When I encourage parents to take their teenagers back into their homes, which means also taking back their children's new and different street identities, I advise caution even as they open the door. No one should feel compromised or in any way at risk in their own home. Having teenagers show their parents new identities doesn't mean children are given permission to walk roughshod over the adults in their lives. We can insist our children's other identities get tidied up so we can accept them into our homes a little more easily.

It is important to make the distinction here that inviting home our children's out-of-home identities is about getting to know who our children really are. But as wonderful as it can be to have a guest stay with us, getting familiar with someone new doesn't have to mean we reject everything old. We don't have to, nor should we, abandon everything we value as our children's caregivers just to accommodate who they want to be.

COMMUNICATION LEADS TO NEGOTIATION

"I'm not going to university next year." In some families, as it was in Sheila's, that was a declaration of war. "I want to go out west, work at a ski hill or tree plant, take some time to travel. But my dad, I'm sure, is gonna freak," Sheila told me one day while meeting her at her school.

"I don't really know how I can tell him. Mom will be okay if he is, otherwise she'll just worry about me."

At eighteen, Sheila's problem is no less daunting than the child who must tell her parents she's pregnant, and that the father is the creepy-looking guy they met when they dragged her from an all-night drunk at a friend's house the week before. In both cases, we parents can be blindsided by what our kids are thinking and doing if we don't stay connected and keep the lines of communication open. Sheila needed her parents' guidance and support even as she made choices they didn't like.

> *No household should have to change to accommodate a young person's street identity. Getting to know our children's risk-taking selves doesn't mean we compromise our integrity. It means only that we accept children for the capacities they show beyond our front doors.*

Sheila had for months been rethinking whether school really fit for her. She'd been drifting towards a peer group that didn't value university, or at least had few expectations that they'd ever go. Sheila's parents had cast questioning looks her way now and again about her choice of friends, but Sheila had brushed them off, or hidden altogether what she was up to. Heck, some of her other friends were beginning to follow her lead and thinking about taking a year off too. In many ways, Sheila was the leader in her pack, the only one thinking outside the box.

"What's the rush with school," she said. "I can get an education later. I've been in school a lot of years already. I have no friggin' clue what to take as my major. I'd be just going to university for my parents. Why?"

I squirmed a little thinking to myself, "If I blow this her parents are going to be ticked off, at me as much as her!"

"I think you've got to talk this over with your parents . . ." I began, hesitant to say too much.

She interrupted me before I could get any further. "I can't talk to them. Dad goes ballistic if I do anything he thinks will embarrass him. Mom doesn't say a word."

I sighed. It was late in the day. We did not have time to talk this through before Sheila went home. Desperate, I said, "I think you need to find a way to convince your parents that this is who you really are. You need to show them you've thought this through, and that it's not as risky as they think. It might be hard to believe, but eventually they'll understand." The sincerity helped ease Sheila's anxiety, but only a little.

"But what do I say?" she asked.

"I'd start with your mom. I'd find an advocate before tackling your dad. Someone who can work behind the scenes. And I wouldn't focus just on the bad stuff, either. It's not like you want to go out west and do nothing. You want to go and work, travel, grow up. Do you see yourself going back to school later?"

"Of course." Her answer didn't surprise me. She was a bright enthusiastic youth who had many interests.

"Will you tell your parents that?" I asked. She gave me an unsteady gaze. "You really need to talk about the positives. You need to show them what you're really about. They need to see you're thinking this through. That doesn't mean that at first they're not going to be upset, but hopefully, they'll see this as part of a whole story of you becoming more who you really are. Different from them. But that's not necessarily bad. You don't have to hide that part of yourself."

She seemed quite happy with what she'd heard and wanted to stay connected with her folks on her terms. One thing was for sure, Sheila didn't want to run away, or feel like she had to abandon her parents to do what she wanted to do. She had always valued them and the advice they had to offer. She had no intention of hurting them, just defending what she believed.

The next time I saw her she was smiling. "It sort of worked," she told me. "They at least said, even my dad said, I could go if I arranged for a job before I go. I've been sending off resumes every day. Dad said I should try the big hotels, places like that. At least to have something to go out to." I would later hear through the grapevine that Sheila's dad was still very upset and anxious his daughter wouldn't return to school. But he had been wise and, rather than putting unnecessary distance between them, had agreed to let her go. My hope was that in time he'd come to value his daughter in the same way others in the community did, as a responsible, level-headed teen. In that way, Sheila reminded me a lot of her parents.

"WHEREFORE ART THOU?"

As it was for Romeo and Juliet, so too is it for many children. They struggle to tell their parents something about themselves that makes them different from others and from their parents. Poor Juliet could never manage to convince her parents that her love for a boy made more sense than their hatred for his family. She may have been taking an awful risk, but she wasn't acting irresponsibly.

In our homes we encounter the combined forces of family, culture, gender, race, class, and the emotional constraints of attachment and belonging. These are all powerful forces that combine to silence our self-expression. The risks we take, with our love, our bodies, and our souls, can be an affront to parents and what they believe.

The challenge, then, for parents, is to create a home environment where there is space for the labels youth construct within their peer groups. The home environment has been called a "holding environment" by psychologist Donald Winnicott.[50] The description is a good one. Home can be a place where a child safely experiments with a new identity and learns the skills necessary to effectively negotiate for acceptance from strangers. Remember, our children want to hear first from us that they belong in our homes, more than out among their peers. They want to know adults see them as trustworthy and responsible. They want to be appreciated for what's special about them, even if those talents are ones we adults tend not to value.

Too often, though, as in Sheila's case, even a healthy family can deny their kids these opportunities to be risk-takers and responsibility-seekers out of fear. That's tragic, really, because these families wind up sending their children out into the world without the survival skills they need to keep themselves safe. They lack the risk-taker's advantage. Surely our homes should be places where they learn the social skills they need to express themselves in responsible, adventuresome ways.

HOME SHOULD BE A PLACE FOR SELF-EXPRESSION

Practically speaking, this means that in our homes there must be space for a child's self-expression. I admit, some of the music blaring from the stereo in my living room makes me cringe. Of course, headphones solve that problem, though I know it might also be worth my while as a parent to take the time to tune in to what my children are listening to.

It all adds up to making the family home a safe place for a child's self-expression. Even if it's only a corner of a bedroom shared with siblings, children need a space in which they can show others who they are. It's the same for adults. I for one have never understood the penchant some of my neighbours have for the ornamental cement figurines that adorn their suburban front lawns. What I can appreciate, however, is that we all need ways to show others who we are, even if not everyone else around us understands our passions or preferences.

When my children were younger, I had the luxury of solving this problem in a house I built by setting aside a small attic room that I half-finished. This was the one room in the house where my children could paint on the walls and floor! Funny how well it worked out, but not in the ways I imagined. I thought I was being clever. I thought they would create cute murals with the fingerpaints I provided. I thought it would be a room I would enjoy looking at as much as they would enjoy creating.

My son and his friends had a different idea. They took black paint and slopped it on just about every surface, making the space seem, to me, sinister and depressing. I found myself horribly disappointed with what they had done, even offering to repaint it all white for them. They looked at me very strangely. "But we like it," they protested. Of course they did. It just took me a while to realize that beyond building the room, my only role was to stand back and let them do with it as they pleased.

Do Something Different

It's time to let go of the fear, to stop fearing the worst, to realize you likely already know how to help your child experience risk and responsibility without serious consequences.

Think back, to the very beginning, when your child was born. Think about all the times you have helped her take risks since then. You helped her stand up. You pushed her on her bike until she pulled away from you, finding her own balance. You left her at the door of her kindergarten classroom, entrusting her to another adult. You let her go on a sleepover. You watched as she learned to cook Kraft Dinner. You've watched her dress ever so self-consciously for her first junior high dance. Maybe you endured her first solo at the wheel of your family car. You've likely helped her through each of these normal transitions with the stalwart love of a good parent, sacrificing your need to keep her safe to her need to grow up.

Unfortunately, for many children, these predictable transitions may not be enough. They want more challenge. More danger.

Remembering those past cherished moments, however, reminds parents to do what we already know how to do well: embrace our children's drive to take risks and become more responsible for themselves and others.

If you need help remembering your past successes, pull out the family album. There amid the cherub-cheeked snapshots is likely the enthusiastic, confident child you as a parent long to nurture. That child didn't happen by accident. You made that child feel safe and secure, gave her the confidence to stand on her own two feet.

Your job isn't over yet.

There are many things one can do to help a child take risks safely and act responsibly. It doesn't really matter where or when you start. Every journey starts with a first step, no matter how late one takes it.

Find the difference that will make the most difference.

Begin with one small change that you are sure will be meaningful to your child. Here's some examples from families I know:

- For the McDaniels, it was letting their daughter drop a science course in high school. She said she wanted to become a business woman, not a scientist.
- For the Duques, it was letting their son use the skateboard park unsupervised.
- For the Thomases, it was letting their daughter travel on her own to see her grandparents.
- For the Henripins, it was letting their son get his eyebrow pierced.
- For the van den Bergs, it was letting their daughter own a hamster, then a goldfish, then a gerbil, a cat, and finally a dog.

What will it be for you and your child? What small gesture will you make that tells your child she is ready for more risk and responsibility? What gesture will be the one that speaks the loudest of the faith you have in her?

LEARNING FROM CHILDREN

If we are to debunk an old myth about all youth who take risks and seek responsibility beyond their years being problem children, then we will need a more powerful story that shows us how things *really* are. The more we understand our children's choices that bring with them messages of hope and belonging, respect and responsibility, the more successful we will be at hearing their truths. Like March storms that signal the impending shift in climate from one season to the next, problem behaviours among our children can be harbingers of resilience when we take the time to hear children's stories told in their own words. Though those behaviours batter us with danger, knock us over with their callousness, and pierce our hearts with their lack of compassion, they are not without meaning. These dangerous, delinquent, deviant, and disordered behaviours are perfectly intelligible solutions our children use to experience risk and responsibility, two building blocks for healthy growth.

We simply can no longer persist in believing that children's pathways to health are dysfunctional when our children behave in ways that trouble us. We must listen closely to our children's accounts of their lives and their elaborate negotiations for opportunities to see themselves as people who belong, are trustworthy, competent, and caring. We must embrace their risk-taking and responsibility-seeking behaviours as normal expressions of their search for an adult-like status. We must stand beside our children and provide them the advantage that comes from exposure to the right amount of risk and responsibility.

ACKNOWLEDGEMENTS

Though there is only one name on the cover of this book, this work is really that of many. First there were the families who shared their stories with me and who were my greatest teachers. And there have been my own family and friends. Most importantly, it has been my partner, Cathy, whose avid reading and critical eye has helped shape so many of the ideas in these pages. There have also been many dinnertime chats with friends who first showed me the need for a book such as this. In particular I need to thank Steve Coughlan and Dale Darling for hosting so many fabulous get-togethers. To them and everyone else who bent my ear, I offer my warmest thanks.

I also owe much to my children, Meg and Scott, who generously showed me how best to parent them and helped me sort out these ideas in the practical world of the everyday.

To my agent, Denise Bukowski, I owe a particular debt for seeing the value of my work and mentoring me through the perils of publishing.

To Susan Renouf, Vice President and Associate Publisher (Non-Fiction) at McClelland & Stewart, I am deeply thankful for her editing that has made this work sound so much better. I also must thank her for the insights she brought to this work from her own life experience as a mother of teens. Her sharing has helped to clarify my thinking in many ways. Many thanks as well to Jenny Bradshaw for her thorough copyedit.

I also need to thank Michele Luchs for her comments on an early draft, as well as Linda Liebenberg and Nora Didkowsky for helping me cope with my many other commitments so that this book could be completed.

Finally, I am indebted to the many authors I cite throughout this work whose efforts have inspired my thinking. I can only hope in some small measure that this work gives something back.

NOTES

1. Vygotsky, L.S. (1978). *Mind in Society: The Development of Higher Psychological Processes.* Edited by M. Cole, V. John-Steiner, S. Scribner and E. Souberman. Cambridge, MA: Harvard University Press.
2. Bauer, G. (September 2005). "Helicopter parents." *Reader's Digest (Canadian Edition).* 131-140.
3. Marano, H.E. (December 2004). "A nation of wimps." *Psychology Today.* 58-70, 103.
4. Ibid. (September/October 2005). "Rocking the cradle of class." *Psychology Today.* 52-58.
5. Guthrie, E. (2002). *The Trouble with Perfect.* New York: Broadway Books. 150.
6. Selner-O'Hagan, M.B., Kindlon, D.J., Buka, S.L., Raudenbush, S.W. & Earls, F.J. (1998). "Assessing exposure to violence in urban youth." *Child Psychology and Psychiatry, 39*(2), 215-224.
7. Davidson, S. & Manion, I.G. (1996). "Facing the challenge: mental health and illness in Canadian youth." *Psychology, Health & Medicine, 1*(1), 41-56; Offord, D.R., Boyle, M.H., Szatmari, P., Rae-Grant, N.I., Links, P.S., Cadman, D.T., Byles, J.A., Crawford, J.W., Blum, H.M., Byrne, C., Thomas, H. & Woodward, C.A. (1987). "Ontario child health study: Six-month prevalence of disorder and rates of service utilization." *Archives of General Psychiatry, 44* (4), 832-836.
8. Popple, P.R. & Leighninger, L. (2005). *Social Work, Social Welfare, and American Society, 6th ed.* New York: Pearson.
9. Cheney, P. (April 23, 2005). *Globe and Mail,* Toronto. F1.

10. The Vanier Institute of the Family (2000). *Profiling Canada's Families II.* Ottawa.

11. Moffitt, T.E. (1997). "Adolescents-limited and life-course-persistent offending: A complementary pair of developmental theories." In T.P. Thornberry (Ed.), *Developmental Theories of Crime and Delinquency* (pp. 11-54). New Brunswick, NJ: Transaction Publishers.

12. Epstein, R. (February 2005). "The loose screw awards." *Psychology Today.* 55-62.

13. Quinn, W.H. (2004). *Family Solutions for Youth at Risk.* New York: Brunner-Routledge.

14. Pittman, K., Irby, M. & Ferber, T. (2001). "Unfinished business: Further reflections on a decade of promoting youth development." In P. Benson & K. Pittman (Eds.), *Trends in Youth Development: Visions, Realities and Challenges* (pp. 3-50). Norwell, MA: Kluwer.

15. Lerner, R.M., Alberts, A.E., Anderson, P.M., & Dowling, E.M. (2006). "On making humans human: spirituality and the promotion of positive youth development." In E.C. Roehlkepartain, P.E. King, L. Wagner, and P. Benson (Eds.), *The Handbook of Spiritual Development in Childhood and Adolescence* (pp. 60-72). Thousand Oaks, CA: Sage Publications.

16. Benson, P.L. (2003). "Developmental assets and asset-building community: Conceptual and empirical foundations." In R.M. Lerner & P.L. Benson (Eds.), *Developmental Assets and Asset-building Communities: Implications for Research, Policy, and Practice* (pp. 19-46). New York: Kluwer.

17. Cited in Damon, W. & Gregory, A. (2003). "Bringing in a new era in the field of youth development." In R.M. Lerner & P.L. Benson (Eds.), *Developmental Assets and Asset-building Communities: Implications for Research, Policy, and Practice* (pp. 47-64). New York: Kluwer.

18. Grossman, L. (January 24, 2005). "Grow up? Not so fast." *Time.* 26-35.

19. Levine, M. (2005). *Ready or Not, Here Life Comes.* New York: Simon and Schuster.

20. Ropeik, D. & Gray, G. (2002). *Risk! A Practical Guide for Deciding What's Really Safe and What's Really Dangerous in the World Around You.* New York: Houghton Mifflin.

21. Perry et al. 1995.

22. Hanson, P.G. (1986). *The Joy of Stress* (Rev. 2nd ed.). Toronto, ON: Hanson Stress Management Organization.

23. Ibid., p. ix.

24. Lightfoot, C. (1997). *The Culture of Adolescent Risk-taking.* New York: Guilford.

25. Masten, A.S. (2001). "Ordinary magic: Resilience processes in development." *American Psychologist, 56*(3), 227-238.

26. Moffitt, T.E. (1997). "Adolescents-limited and life-course-persistent offending: A complementary pair of developmental theories." In T.P. Thornberry (Ed.), *Developmental Theories of Crime and Delinquency* (pp. 11-54). New Brunswick, NJ: Transaction Publishers.

27. Tremblay, R., Boulerice, B., Harden, P.W., McDuff, P., Pérusse, D., Pihl, R.O., Zoccolillo, M. (1996). *Do Children in Canada Become More Aggressive as They Approach Adolescence?* In Human Resources Development Canada & Statistics Canada (Eds.), *Growing Up in Canada: National Longitudinal Survey of Children and Youth.* Ottawa: Statistics Canada.

28. De Graaf, J., Wann, D., Naylor, T.H. (2001). *Affluenza: The All-consuming Epidemic.* San Francisco: Berrett-Koehler.

29. Luthar, S.S. & Latendresse, S.J. (2002). "Adolescent risk: The costs of affluence." In R.M. Lerner, C.S. Taylor & A. Von Eye (Eds.), *Pathways to Positive Development Among Diverse Youth* (pp. 101-122). New York: Jossey-Bass.

30. Chesney-Lind, M. & Belknap, J. (2004). "Trends in delinquent girls' aggression and violent behavior: A review of the evidence." In M. Putallaz & K.L. Bierman (Eds.), *Aggression, Antisocial Behavior, and Violence Among Girls: A Developmental Perspective* (pp. 203-221). New York: Guilford.

31. Derrida, J. (1978). *Writing and Difference.* Chicago: University of Chicago.

32. Ladner, J.A. (1971). *Tomorrow's Tomorrow: The Black Woman.* Garden City, NY: Anchor Books; Robinson, R.A. (1994). "Private pain and public behaviors: Sexual abuse and delinquent girls." In C.K. Riessman (Ed.), *Qualitative Studies in Social Work Research* (pp. 73-94). Thousand Oaks, CA: Sage; Taylor, J.M., Gilligan, C. & Sullivan, A.M. (1995). *Between Voice and Silence: Women and Girls, Race and Relationship.* Cambridge, MA: Harvard University Press.

33. Giroux, H.A. (2002). "The war on the young: Corporate culture, schooling, and the politics of 'zero tolerance.'" In R. Strickland (Ed.), *Growing up Postmodern: Neoliberalism and the War on the Young* (pp. 35-46). New York: Rowman and Littlefield.

34. *Time* (August 8, 2005). "Being 13." 30-35.

35. Stone, I. (1961). *The Agony and the Ecstasy.* New York: Doubleday.

36. Winnicott, D.W. (1965). *The Maturational Process and the Facilitating Environment.* New York: International Universities Press.

37. Miller, J.B. (1976). *Toward a New Psychology of Women.* Boston, MA: Beacon Press.

38. Gilligan, C. (1982). *In a Different Voice: Psychological Theory and Women's Development.* Cambridge, MA: Harvard University Press.

39. Osherson, S. (1992). *Wrestling with Love: How Men Struggle with Intimacy with Women, Children, Parents and Each Other.* New York: Fawcett Columbine.

40. Ross, T., Conger, D. & Armstrong, M. (2002). "Bridging child welfare and juvenile justice: Preventing unnecessary detention of foster children." *Child Welfare, 81*(3), 471-494; Loeber, R., Farrington, D.P., Stouthamer-Loeber, M., & Van Kammen, W.B. (1998). "Multiple risk factors for multi-problem boys: Co-occurrence of delinquency, substance use, attention deficit, conduct problems, physical aggression, covert behavior, depressed mood, and shy/withdrawn behavior." In R. Jessor (Ed.) *New Perspectives in Adolescent Risk Behaviour.* New York: Cambridge University Press; Murphy, R.A. (2002) "Mental Health, Juvenile Justice, and Law Enforcement Responses to Youth Psychopathology." In D.T. Marsh and M.A. Fristad (Eds.) *Handbook of Serious Emotional Disturbance in Children and Adolescents* (pp. 351-374). New York: John Wiley & Sons, Inc.

41. Zimmerman, M.A. (1990). "Toward a theory of learned hopefulness: A structural model analysis of participation and empowerment." *Journal of Research in Personality, 24,* 71-86.

42. Hall, G.S. (1904). *Adolescence, Vols 1 & 2.* New York: Appleton.

43. Arnett, J.J. (1999). "Adolescent storm and stress, reconsidered." *American Psychologist, 54*(5), 317-326.

44. Miles, S. (2000). *Youth Lifestyles in a Changing World.* Buckingham, UK: Open University Press.

45. Schissel, B., op. cit.

46. Tyyskä, V. (2001). *Long and Winding Road: Adolescents and Youth in Canada Today.* Toronto, ON: Canadian Scholars' Press.

47. White, M. (2000). "Re-engaging with history: The absent by implicit." *Reflections on Narrative Practice: Essays & Interviews.* Adelaide, AU: Dulwich Centre Publications.

48. de Shazar, S. (1985). *Keys to Solutions in Brief Therapy.* New York: Norton.

49. Gellatt, H.B. *Creative Decision Making: Using Positive Uncertainty.* Oakville, Ontario: Reid Publishing, 1991.

50. Winnicott, D.W., op cit.

INDEX

teachers: arguments with parents, 29; as role models, 140; questions to ask self, 17–18
teenagers *see* youth
timing, of risk-taking, 86, 88, 91
tolerance, *99*, 100
ToughLove approach, 112–13
trauma, 44, 69, *156–57*
travel: and experiencing different communities and cultures, *47–48*, *99*; as rite of passage, 85; by child or youth alone, 10, 55, 74, 85–86
Tremblay, Richard, 80
trial and error, 72

United Nations, on child rights, 20
United States, child protection laws, 20

violence: and adjusting parenting style appropriately, 68; children experiencing, 131; current statistics, 105–6; real vs. perceived, 102; today vs. yesterday, 18–19
volunteering, 67, *94–95*
Vygotsky, Lev, 3

war, and children, 46, 57–58, 130–31, 196–97
wealth: and giving children what they really need, 92–93; and push for conformity, 132; as threat to children's happiness, *89–91*; predictor of drug use, *89–90*
White, Michael, 182
Wilson, Mary Ellen, 20
Winnicott, Donald, 151

work: deaths on the job, 22; importance to child's growth, 49–50, *89*, 93, *94–95*; injuries on the job, 22; in non-mainstream or non-North American cultures, 51, 130–31; today vs. yesterday, 20

York, David, 112
York, Phyllis, 112
youth, *see also* children: angry, 148–51; anxiety among, 15; as scapegoats for social ills, 180–81; awkwardness about relationship with parents, 145; communicating with parents about risk-taking, 87; contributing to community, 93, 170–71; contributing to family, *145*; control negotiations, 145–46; cost of affluence, *89–90*; death of, through dangerous choices, 164–70; depression among, 15; drug use, 5–8; in other countries, 49; living with parents, 23, 49; need for connections, 143, 145, 151–52, 164; need to be noticed, 172, 184–85; need to feel competent, 171–72; not necessarily in need of conflict, 174–75; resilience of those "at risk," 79–80; sanctions toward, 106–7; seeking control over mind, body, spirit, 80–81, *83–84*; seeking self-expression, 180–81; suicide attempts, 6; taking risks as a game, 73; today vs. yesterday, 180–81; work deaths and injuries, 22

ABOUT THE AUTHOR

Michael Ungar is an internationally recognized expert on resilience in at-risk youth and leads the International Resilience Project that includes researchers in eleven countries. He is a professor at the School of Social Work at Dalhousie University and runs a private practice specializing in working with children and adults in mental health and correctional settings. He has lectured extensively on the subject of resilience and is the author of four books and dozens of professional and scholarly articles. Michael Ungar lives in Halifax with his wife and two children.